THE 75 GREATEST

MANAGEMENT

DECISIONS

EVER MADE

...AND SOME OF THE WORST.

**BUSINESS LEADERS TALK
ABOUT THE GOOD AND THE BAD**

STUART CRAINER

MJF BOOKS
NEW YORK

This publication is designed to provide accurate and authoritative information in regard to the subject matter covered. It is sold with the understanding that the publisher is not engaged in rendering legal, accounting, or other professional service. If legal advice or other assistance is required, the services of a competent professional person should be sought.

Published by MJF Books
Fine Communications
322 Eighth Avenue
New York, NY 10001

The 75 Greatest Management Decisions Ever Made
LC Control Number 2002106257
ISBN 1-56731-532-1

Manufactured in the United States of America on acid-free paper ∞

MJF Books and the MJF colophon are trademarks of Fine Creative Media, Inc.

BG   10   9   8   7   6   5   4   3   2   1

Contents

Introduction

Amid the fanfares being prepared for the new millennium, there are numerous listings and rankings of the great and the good. Most selections feature scientists, writers, artists, sports personalities, media stars, and entertainers. Their achievements, inspirations, and personalities are pored over and celebrated. Managers are conspicuous by their absence. Yet management is one of the great triumphs of our age. In the twentieth century, humanity discovered management as a discipline, as a profession, and sometimes as a calling.

Of course, management is nothing new. Napoleon was exercising management when he deployed his forces. The ancient Egyptians practiced management when they built the pyramids. The teams of gardeners cultivating the Hanging Gardens of Babylon did not simply turn up and do whatever first came to mind. They were managed. A steady stream of books even attest that Jesus Christ was a manager (witness the book, *Jesus CEO*). "Jesus taught many great principles," says Charles Manz, author of *The Leadership Wisdom of Jesus*. "A good actual decision was when he told anyone who had not sinned to throw the first stone in stoning a woman caught in adultery, and by doing so chose not to condemn but to forgive."

Indeed, the Bible is a ready source of management decisions. "By deciding to divide people into their tens, hundreds, and thousands, Moses was the first to establish a hierarchy, a chain of command," observes the University of Southern California's Warren Bennis. Think of Noah, the project manager, making weighty logistical decisions within a tight and immovable deadline. "Could we include Joseph's advice to the

Pharaoh on planting wheat to store for seven years?" asked Philip Kotler of Northwestern's Kellogg School when the question of nominating a decision was put to him. "Or Jesus' choice of his twelve disciples (except the blunder of Judas)? One could play with the question for years."

The more you look for great management decisions, the more you see. None of the great monuments of history would exist if it weren't for management. The Italian painters of the Renaissance may have been artistic geniuses, but they were also shrewd managers, able to take advantage of delegation. The teams of laborers who helped build London's St. Paul's Cathedral did not gather spontaneously; they were recruited and managed.

Inevitably, some monuments are testimony to bad management. The Leaning Tower of Pisa would not attract tourists if it were perfectly vertical. For this edifice we can thank a thirteenth-century Italian building supervisor, a manager by any other title.

The somewhat daunting reality is that virtually all decisions we make are managerial in nature. Decisions usually concern people (human resources); money (budgeting); buying and selling (marketing); how to do things (operations); or what to do in the future (strategy and planning). The obvious exceptions are emotional decisions, though some sad creatures actually bring analysis to bear on their choice of partner. The University of Oklahoma's Daniel Wren, coauthor of *Management Innovators,* notes the decision made by scientific management champion Frank Gilbreth to marry Lillian Moller, and their subsequent decision to have twelve children. The Gilbreths, made famous by the book *Cheaper by the Dozen* (later made into a film) were early advocates of working smarter, not harder. They truly practiced what they preached, running their household according to their theories. (This is akin to Michael Porter having five children to prove the five forces framework, or Tom Peters having seven children whose names begin with *S*.)

While management is a truly human science, it is interesting that people-related decisions are generally not the ones that remain strongly imprinted in peoples' minds. Indeed, the most-cited great decision makers are Henry Ford and Bill Gates—two managers not exactly renowned for their people management skills. Instead, people remember decisions that change businesses, industries, and history.

Curiously, while management is eternal and all-embracing, the debate continues to rage about what actually constitutes management. (It should be noted that the debate usually rages in academia, not on factory floors.) The host of definitions now available cannot cloud the central fact that management is about decision making. "Decisions are the essence of management," says Des Dearlove, author of *Key Management Decisions*. "Management without decision making is a vacuum. Of course, that does not mean that every decision a manager makes is important or that managers always make the right decisions. The vast majority of decisions made by managers are completely unimportant. And often the decisions they make are the wrong ones."

Managers are not perfect, but who ever said that management was about perfection? The reality is that management is about a combination of following inexplicable hunches, getting lucky, working hard, and taking risks. Often managers fall on their faces. That's part of the job. Managers may run all the data through the latest regression analysis software and still screw up the decision. For every great decision, there are hundreds that didn't quite work out.

There is a wafer-thin line between success and failure. The division is often barely discernible: Will Apple go down in history as the company that invented an industry, or as a glorious failure that had a fantastic product but not the foresight to build long-term success?

The roots of successful decisions often lie in obscure places. Peter Cohan, author of *Technology Leaders,* cites as an example the story of how Hewlett-Packard found itself in the inkjet printer business. In the late 1970s, H-P's Vancouver, WA division was in trouble. It had few products and management was considering whether to fold it into another division. One of the engineers, working in a converted janitor's closet, had discovered that if metal was heated in a specific way, it splattered all over the room. The engineers realized that this discovery could be the basis for a new way to spray ink onto a page. Richard Hackborn, an H-P executive, told the division manager that exploiting this discovery was his last chance to save the Vancouver division. Ten years later, this decision proved to be the basis for over $6 billion in H-P revenues.

Success comes out of the closet and can also emerge from apparent failure. Our list includes examples of companies that made catastrophic errors but then retrieved the situation. Writer and bookseller Ted Kinni cites Johnson & Johnson's 1982 decision to pull Tylenol from store shelves as a classic. "They put customer safety before corporate profit," says Kinni. (Warren Bennis provides another interesting slant: "Johnson & Johnson CEO, Jim Burke, was the first corporate leader to recognize the significance of the media. Tylenol was about being totally up front and public.") Likewise the new-recipe Coke fiasco. The classic wrong decision—to tinker with a hugely successful product—was soon replaced by an admission of error and the introduction of Classic Coke. Many managers would have blindly stuck with the original decision to make the change.

Sometimes, perhaps once or twice in their careers, managers get it gloriously right. In 1950 Frank McNamara found himself in a restaurant with no money. After phoning his wife for help, McNamara came up with the idea of the Diners Club Card, which was launched among 27 Manhattan restaurants. Within a year the club had 42,000 members and the credit card was born.

Getting it right usually has nothing to do with the software package working properly. Bill Gates didn't need decision-making software when he ceded control of the license to use MS/DOS for the IBM PC while remaining in control of the license for all non-IBM PCs. When Compaq, Dell, Hewlett-Packard, and Gateway took over the PC market from IBM, Gates had locked in the foundation on which his wealth is built. Great decision, Bill.

The truly great decisions just happen. They are the stuff of spur-of-the-moment phone calls, crazy ideas tried when you are desperate, schemes that emerge out of the corporate ether. Even the strategy gurus are all too ready to admit that strategy is fatally flawed by the messiness of reality. "I am a professor of strategy and oftentimes I am ashamed to admit it," confesses Gary Hamel, coauthor of *Competing for the Future,* "because there is a dirty secret: We know a great strategy when we see one. In business schools we teach them and pin them to the wall. They are specimens. Most of our smart students raise their hands and say, 'Wait a minute, was that luck or foresight?' They're partly right. We don't have a theory of strategy creation. There is no foundation beneath the multibillion-dollar strategy industry. Strategy is lucky foresight. It comes from a serendipitous cocktail."[1]

At their moment of triumph—as serendipity kicks in and everything turns rosy—it is unlikely that managers shout, "Eureka!" Breaking into foreign languages during board meetings is not a recommended path forward in your career. Nor do managers crack open a bottle of champagne or slide naked down the banisters into a reception hall, whistling "Stairway to Heaven."

Managers tend not to celebrate when decisions are gloriously justified, for two reasons. First, getting it right is part of the job. Managers are paid to do the right thing (and, according to *Dilbert*, blame others if they fail to do so). If you have screwed up the launch of your product in Estonia and Latvia, it seems excessive to celebrate when you make a perfect entry into the Finnish market.

Second, managers do not celebrate getting it right because usually they do not even realize they have gotten it right. It is one of the great disappointments of life that perfect decisions are usually only perfect in retrospect. Henry Ford did not sprint around Detroit announcing the arrival of mass production. Queen Isabella of Spain did not immediately proclaim her wisdom when she sponsored Columbus' sail into the distance. She sensibly kept quiet. (The corollary lesson is to beware of anyone who trumpets the perfection of a decision. If Queen Isabella had handed out a press release announcing the imminent discovery of America, you can be sure that America would still lie undiscovered.)

Managerial decision are risks. In hindsight they may seem obvious. Of course, Intel had to get out of the memory business. International Business Machines? Bound to be globally successful. Mickey? Great name for a cartoon mouse. But did Walt Disney know that he would make many millions of dollars from a cartoon mouse? Did he know it was an important decision at the time? I don't think so. It wasn't a foolproof scheme to get rich quick, just a decision that worked.

Today's success story is yesterday's risky decision. London Business School's Don Sull selects GE's choice of Jack Welch to succeed Reg Jones as a great decision precisely for this reason. "We forget now that it was considered a high-risk decision at the time," says Sull.

THE MEANING OF DECISIONS

"The essence of ultimate decision remains impenetrable to the observer—often indeed, to the decider himself. . . . There will always be the dark and tangled stretches in the decision-making process—mysterious even to those who may be most intimately involved," said John F Kennedy.[2]

An air of mystery lies at the heart of decisions and decision making. An entire academic discipline, decision science, is devoted to understanding management decision making. Much of the theory is built on the foundations set down by early business thinkers, who believed that under a given set of circumstances human behavior was logical and therefore predictable. The fundamental belief of the likes of computer pioneer Charles Babbage and Scientific Management founder Frederick Taylor was that the decision process (and many other things) could be rationalized and systematized. Based on this premise, models were developed to explain the workings of commerce, and the same models were applied to the way in which decisions are made.

Belief in decision theory persists. Indeed, most management books and ideas are inextricably linked to helping managers make better decisions. Strategic management, for example, was a model by which strategic decisions could be made. Unfortunately, it was a model that demanded vast amounts of data. As a result, enthusiastic managers turned themselves into data addicts rather than better decision makers. Decisions were perpetually delayed as more data was gathered in order to ensure the decision would be 100 percent certain to work. "Paralysis by analysis" became commonplace.

Now a profusion of models, software packages, and analytical tools promise to distill decision making into a formula. Decision-making models assume that the distilled mass of experience will enable people to make accurate decisions that incorporate learning from other peoples' experiences. Many promise the world: Feed in your particular circumstances and out will pop an answer. The danger is in concluding that the solution provided by a software package is the *best* answer.

Whether embedded in a software package or buried in a textbook, decision theorizing suggests that effective decision making involves a number of logical stages. This is referred to as the "rational model of decision making" or the "synoptic model." This involves a series of steps: identifying the problem; clarifying the problem; prioritizing goals; generating options; evaluating options (using appropriate analysis); comparing predicted outcomes of each option with the goals; and choosing the option that best matches the goals. These models rely on a number of assumptions about the way people will behave when confronted with a set of circumstances. The assumptions allow mathematicians to derive formulas based on probability theory. Some decision-making tools include features such as cost–benefit analysis, which purports to help managers evaluate different options.

Alluring though they are, the trouble with decision-making theories is that reality is often more confused and messy than a neat model can allow for. Underpinning the mathematical approach are a number of flawed assumptions, such as that decision making is consistent, based on accurate information, free from emotion or prejudice, and rational. Another obvious drawback to any decision-making model is that identifying what you need to make a decision about is often more important than making the actual decision itself. If a decision seeks to solve a problem, it may be the right decision but the wrong problem.

The reality is that managers make decisions based on a combination of intuition, experience, and analysis. Because intuition and experience are impossible to measure in any sensible way, the temptation is to focus on the analytical side of decision making, the science rather than the mysterious art. (The entire management consultancy industry is based on reaching decisions through analysis.) Of course, managers in the real world do not care whether they are practicing an art or a science. What they care about is solving problems and reaching reliable, well-informed decisions.

This does not mean that decision theory is redundant or that decision-making models should be cast to one side. Indeed, a number of factors have rendered decision making ever more demanding. The growth in complexity means that companies no longer encounter simple problems. Complex decisions are now not simply the preserve of the most senior managers but the responsibility of many others in organizations. In addition, managers have to deal with a flood of information: A survey by Reuters of 1,200 managers worldwide found that 43 percent thought important decisions were delayed and their ability to make decisions was affected as a result of having too much information.

These factors suggest that any techniques, models, or analyses that enable managers to make more informed decisions more quickly will be in increasing demand. In the past, models were the domain of economists and strategists. Now, there is increasing use of decision support systems in other fields. Some show the best types of decisions for a given situation. Typically, these involve how best to use resources. An oil refinery, for example, might use a support system to determine on a daily basis the optimum amount of product it should produce. Airlines run similar programs to establish optimum pricing levels. Other systems promise to yield increasingly better decisions based on past results. These learning-based models allow companies to take the data they have gathered and any analysis they have undertaken and gather them up in one place, directly related to the decision.

There is little doubt that decision theory and the use of decision-making models can be falsely reassuring. They can lend legitimacy to decisions that are based on prejudices or hunches. The usefulness of decision-making models remains a leap of faith. None are foolproof, because none are universally applicable. And none can yet cope with the willful idiosyncrasies of human behavior.

SELECTING THE GREATS

This celebration of the 75 greatest management decisions is drawn from throughout the ages and throughout the world. Executives, consultants, academics, commentators, and opinionated people from the business world and elsewhere were canvassed for their ideas and insights. As you would expect, opinions and suggestions on which decisions to include varied greatly.

Jim Collins, coauthor of *Built to Last,* chose seven key decisions:

- Boeing's bet on the 707 in the 1950s.

- GE's decision to build the world's first industrial research and development laboratory early in the twentieth century.

- Procter & Gamble's invention of brand management.

- 3M's decision to allow its scientists to spend 15 percent of their time working on anything they want.

- Motorola's decision to get out of all its original businesses in the 1960s, as a step to force itself to begin a process of continual renewal.

- Philip Morris' decision to reposition a woman's cigarette with a macho image and a cowboy ad campaign.

- Sony's decision to write a philosophical prospectus before it had products to sell.

Others looked further backward. "One of my favorites is General Douglas MacArthur's decision to rebuild the Japanese economy, particularly telecommunications. He could have decided otherwise, but that fateful decision would lead to Deming and Juran going to Japan, turning that country into a formidable competitor," said Daniel Wren.

Peter Cohan, author of *Technology Leaders*, suggested a number of great decisions. They included John D. Rockefeller's decision to stabilize the price of oil by buying up all the refining capacity, and then using his purchasing power to lock up low-cost railroad transportation deals. "These related decisions helped make Rockefeller history's richest person," said Cohan. Others he mentioned included Jeff Bezos' decision to use the Internet to sell books through Amazon.com.

Alex Knight of Ashridge Consulting suggested I look at the great and the good. His choices for great decisions included Peter the Great's decision to change Russia without ever telling anyone that he had a vision; Mikhail Gorbachev's decision to end the Cold War (by the roundabout route of telling then President George Bush while in a helicopter traveling to Camp David that he would never press the nuclear button); and Nelson Mandela for his decision to make Chief Butelezi, his archenemy, president of South Africa for three days while he and Thabo Mbeki attended a world conference for leaders.

The resulting selection of decisions is as eclectic and eccentric as you would expect. The link between the 75, which may seem tenuous at times, is simply that all the decisions were successful and all had a wide impact.

The actual moment in time when a decision is made is often not entirely clear. "It is a perplexing fact that most executive decisions produce no direct evidence of themselves and that knowledge of them can only be derived from the cumulation of indirect evidence," wrote early management thinker, Chester Barnard. "They must largely be inferred from general results in which they are merely one factor, and from symptomatic indications of roundabout character."[3]

Decisions tend to emerge from surrounding events as much as from grand announcements. Charles Moore spent four years carrying out research at United Parcel Service and concluded that good decisions take a lot of time; combine the efforts of a number of people; give individuals the freedom to dissent; are reached without any pressure from the top to achieve an artificial consensus; and are made with the participation of those responsible for implementing them.[4]

Henry Mintzberg has defined a decision as "commitment to action" and observed that "many decisions cannot easily be pinned down, in time or in place." This selection of decisions is geared toward the word *action*.[5] The decisions collected here made things happen. The greatest decisions change things. They change industries. And, in doing so, they change our lives.

Some decisions change our lives, by setting standards, creating models for behavior. "I would nominate the decision by Aaron Feuerstein of Malden Mills in 1995 to keep his business open in the wake of a major fire that destroyed most of his company," says Charles Manz. Feuerstein kept his entire workforce of 2,400 people on the payroll and paid them out of his own pocket. "Most people would've been happy at their seventieth birthday to take the insurance money and go to Florida, but I don't want to do that," Feuerstein said. His decision appeared to be bad business at the time, even though it was highly moral. In the end, Malden Mills was back to virtually full capacity within 90 days. The committed and grateful workforce worked so well that productivity shot up. Feuerstein concluded that they paid him back nearly tenfold.

Feuerstein's decision had everything: high risk, strong ethics, humanity, and a business payoff. It is proof that decision making is not only the heart of management; it is the heartbeat of life. Decision making is living. Managers live to decide and decide to make a living.

USING THIS BOOK

The 75 Greatest Management Decisions Ever Made is organized—or disorganized—under ten headings:

- Industry Inventors
- The Name Game
- Supermodels
- Getting On

- Marketing Magic
- Lucky Foresight
- Leading by Example

- Competitive Advantages
- Bright Ideas
- People Power

The 75 greats are followed by a collection of not-so-greats, a reminder that adversity is more common in life, and certainly in business life, than triumph. The entries for the decisions, great and bad, vary in length and are drawn from throughout history. The beauty is in the eclectic mix. No such collection could hope to be comprehensive or even authoritative. All it can do is tell some interesting stories and extrapolate their usefulness for today's manager. I hope that the end result is a cornucopia of instructive management decisions, past and present.

Notes

[1] International Management Symposium, London Business School, October, 1997.

[2] Allison, Graham T., *Essence of Decision: Explaining the Cuban Missile Crisis*, Little Brown, 1971.

[3] Barnard, Chester, *The Function of the Executive*, Harvard University Press, 1970.

[4] Foreman, Charles, "Managing a decision into being," Management Course for Presidents.

[5] Mintzberg, Henry; Langley, Ann; Pitcher, Patricia; Posada, Elizabeth; and Saint-Macary, Jan, "Opening up decision making: the view from the black stool," *Organization Science*, May-June 1995.

BOOKS ON DECISION MAKING

Baron, Jonathan, *Thinking and Deciding*, 2nd ed., Cambridge University Press, 1994.

Dearlove, Des, *Key Management Decisions*, FT/Pitman, 1997.

Faust, Gerald W., Lyles, Richard I., and Phillips, Will, *Responsible Managers Get Results*, AMACOM, 1998.

French, Simon, *Decision Theory: An Introduction to the Mathematics of Rationality*, Ellis Horwood and John Wiley, 1988.

Keeney, Ralph L., *Value-Focused Thinking: A Path to Creative Decision Making*, Harvard University Press, 1992.

Richards, Max D., & Greenlaw, Paul S., *Management Decision Making*, Richard D. Irwin Inc., 1996.

Yates, J. Frank, *Judgment and Decision Making*, Prentice Hall, 1990.

ACKNOWLEDGMENTS

The genesis of this book was an article I wrote for the *Management Review*, a publication of the American Management Association. The article was the idea of Barbara Ettorre, the magazine's editor. I am grateful to Barbara for her initial inspiration and for those who helped with the article at the magazine. The person who picked up the baton after the article was published was Adrienne Hickey of AMACOM. I thank her for her decisiveness in moving the idea forward so speedily, as well as for her editorial input and insight.

A wide variety of opinions were canvassed to collect *The 75 Greatest Management Decisions Ever Made*. I am grateful to all who participated, and in particular to Philip Kotler of Northwestern; Don Sull and Costas Markides of London Business School; Chris Lederer and Sam Hill of Helios Consulting; Peter Cohan; Alex Knight and Phil Hodgson of Ashridge Management College; David Arnold of Harvard Business School; Warren Bennis and Jay Conger of the University of Southern California; Charles Manz; Randy White of RPW Executive Development; William E. Halal of George Washington University; Daniel Wren of the University of Oklahoma; and Ann Marucheck and Allison Adams of Kenan-Flagler.

Thanks also go to Gerry Griffin of Burson Marsteller for his insistence that Elvis had to be included, and to Des Dearlove for his seamanship.

Particular thanks go to Stephen Coomber, who carried out a great deal of research and gathered a huge amount of material on each of these great decisions and many more.

STUART CRAINER
March 1999

The 75 Greatest Management Decisions Ever Made

THE 75
GREATEST
MANAGEMENT
DECISIONS
EVER MADE

INDUSTRY INVENTORS

In 1961 Jean Nidetch was put on a diet by the Obesity Clinic at the New York Department of Health. She invited six dieting friends to meet with her in her Queens apartment every week. That decision created Weight Watchers and the diet industry.

Few can lay claim to truly creating a new industry. Those that do so know that their place in the pantheon of business greats is probably secure. Create an industry and corporate Mount Rushmore beckons. But though many are called, few are chosen.

Sometimes it looks easy. In the nineteenth century, Andrew Carnegie decided to import British steel and steelmaking processes to America to build railway bridges made of steel instead of wood. The imported skills ignited the U.S. steel industry, and Carnegie became a steel baron.

The bad news is that, having created an industry, business life may then be all downhill. From the top, it is a long descent into the morass of ordinariness. Corporate life at the top is fickle and short-lived. Enjoy the glory if and when you can.

Great Decision #1

In Thebes in 100 BC someone lost a slave named Shem. The owner decided to post an advertisement offering "a whole gold coin" for the slave's return. This is the oldest existing ad and the precursor of the modern advertising merry-go-round.

Advertising is one of the phenomena of the twentieth century. There is no escape from its all-pervasive attempts at persuasion. Try walking down a street without encountering advertising in any of its million formats. It is impossible: Taxis are now festooned with advertisements, billboards proclaim their messages on every scrap of land, airships hover overhead with messages from their sponsors, and the school crossing guard wears a coat that displays a car manufacturer's logo. Museums even have exhibitions of advertisements of the past that we know and love. And it all began with Shem.

Technology only serves to make advertising even more inescapable. Supermarkets are already testing a device that is triggered as you walk down the aisle, pondering your next purchase. As you approach the cat food, a voice encourages you to buy a particular brand. The Internet may be a great vehicle for communication, but it is also the ultimate global advertising medium.

Amid the celebrations of how clever advertisers are or nostalgia for a bygone age of consumer innocence, it is easy to forget that advertising is everywhere because it works. Advertising sells. It is glamorous, creative, eye-catching, and expensive, but it is nothing unless it increases sales of a product or service.

We may say we are unimpressed, not persuaded by the claims that Tide washes clothes whiter or that Heineken refreshes parts of our bodies we didn't know existed, but the images and slogans remain ingrained in our consciousness for decades. We remember; then we buy.

Advertising is all about boosting the bottom line but, along the way, advertisements have become cultural reference points. We buy records simply because they have been used in TV campaigns and the characters featured in advertisements are enduring fixtures in our lives. Even Budweiser's frogs were lovable. (Frogs, for some reason, usually are.)

The roots of mass media advertising lie in the United States. The United States is home of the USP, the Unique Selling Proposition. Its most famous proponent was Rosser Reeves, the doyen of New York's advertising heart, Madison Avenue. According to a famous story, a client came into Reeves' office and cast two new coins onto the desk. "Mine is the one on the left. You prove it's better," challenged the client. This is the basic problem facing anyone in advertising. Proving "It's better" is their job, whether they are handling an account for dog food or trying to persuade you to open a pension plan with a particular bank. Rosser Reeves was usually up to the task. He dreamed up "It cleans your breath while it cleans your teeth" for Colgate Dental Cream, a slogan that allowed Colgate to lead the market for decades; and "Helps you break the laxative habit" for Carter's Little Liver Pills. Most controversially, he helped sell Eisenhower to the people in the 1952 presidential campaign.

Today the power of advertising is accepted and exploited by a huge variety of businesses. The list of big spenders is broadening. The skeptical might suggest that advertising should have no place in selling presidential candidates or pension plans. In reply, the advertising industry usually retorts that advertising is a powerful means of communication, as well as overt persuasion. Indeed, limits on advertising are increasingly hard to find.

Advertising has become absorbed under the umbrella of branding. The roots of some of the world's leading brands can be traced back to an early willingness to invest in advertising. Advertising is at the front line of brand warfare. Advertising is now so omnipresent it is little wonder that it increasingly finds itself embroiled in controversy. Of course, controversy can be used to stimulate debate and sell products; consider the Benneton ads that wear their hearts and their issues on their sleeves. Is this legitimate consciousness awakening, as the company claims, or a crass shock tactic to imprint the Benneton name on our minds? Advertising is increasingly targeted at our consciences. One bank uses an advertisement showing a bird covered in oil. Its message is that the bank invests its money ethically. The secondary message is, "Open an account with us and you can stop the suffering of animals."

Such advertising can be seen as stirring up legitimate debate or as taking things too far. Maurice Saatchi has warned against the suppression of creativity in advertising: "Directives on broadcasting. Restrictions on advertising. Bans on sexual stereotyping. Where will it end? Presumably, objections will be raised in due course to the advertising of washing powder, on the grounds that people should not be duped into the dangerous belief that they can dirty their clothes and get away with it."

The debate over the responsibility of advertisers is broadening. The Canadian courts decided that bans on cigarette advertising are infringements on free speech. The question must be where free speech reaches its limitations.

Given the ability of advertising to generate often unwanted controversy, it is little wonder that there is a current fashion for retro-advertising that harkens back to the tasteless, but noncontroversial, triumphs of the past. Fashions come, go, and—even in our lifestyle-fixated times—reappear. That does not mean that clever or intensive advertising can turn failure into success. The bottom line remains the same: Advertising can promise the world, but it always has to deliver results; it can shock or inform, but it still has to sell.

THE GREATEST LESSONS

Advertising remains mysterious.   Advertising works. Of course it does. But, famously, the problem lies in deciding which advertising works and in which ways. The mystery adds to the allure of the trade (and we will never know whether or not Shem was found).

Advertising can never be completely uniform.   Advertising's power and reach are now truly global, with advertising campaigns aimed at entire continents rather than individual countries. The attractions are simple. If the same advertisement that works in Italy will work in Finland, you don't need to make two. (Of course, working in foreign languages produces predictable troubles, which should never be underestimated. Nike's "Just do it" slogan, for example, cannot be easily translated into French. The compromise is the French slogan, "Ta vie est à toi," or "Your life is your own.") Research by Jean-Noel Kapferer of Groupe ESC in France found that 29 percent of companies have globalized their advertising. Some, like Nike and Gillette, make global advertisements with small local adaptations. It is the same but slightly different, especially for you, and you, and you.

The potential pitfalls of global advertising are many, varied, and often overlooked. Legislation is a minefield. In France, for example, supermarket gas stations cannot advertise on television, thanks to a ban on advertising by the distribution sector. Then there are cultural factors. Research by market research company Mintel indicated that 22 percent of French people are likely to sample a product if it is endorsed by a celebrity. The British remain studiously unimpressed; only one percent said they would be influenced by a celebrity. This, of course, begs the question as to why television advertisements in the U.K. consistently employ a host of minor celebrities.

Great Decision #2

Apple's decision to chase the prize of the first saleable PC created an industry. The Apple 1 led to Apple 2, then to VisiCalc, and finally to the Mac, first shipped in 1984. Apple's decision also drew a veil over Xerox's decision not to go ahead with development after its PARC team had made a vital breakthrough.

When Apple launched the iMac, the stylish Internet-ready computer it hoped would reenergize the company's fading fortunes, "Chic, not geek" was emblazoned across advertising posters. Beneath those words were the Apple logo and the slogan, "Think different." The campaign epitomized the enduring appeal of Apple.

Like all the best computer companies, Apple began life in a garage. In 1977, Steve Jobs conceived the Apple 1, regarded by many as the first real personal computer. Jobs and his technically brilliant partner, Steve Wozniak, built the first machine in a garage. They founded the Apple Company. The Apple 2 followed, and then the Apple Macintosh.

For a time, Apple was quite simply the hippest thing in computers and corporate America. The key decision that drove the company was to make computers accessible to ordinary people. The company succeeded and did so with style. In a market in which design went no further than beige boxes, the Apple machines stood out from the crowd.

Instead of writing commands in computerese, Apple owners used a mouse to click on easily recognizable icons—a trash can and file folders, for example. Suddenly, you didn't need a degree in computer science to operate a personal computer. Other companies followed where Apple led, most significantly Microsoft. But while Apple remained the darling of the creative world, Bill Gates and crew never achieved the same iconoclast status. Maybe Microsoft would have been more loved if it too had begun life in a garage.

For a while Apple managed to scoop up 20 percent of the market. Ownership of an Apple machine was a statement of identity: It was jeans and sneakers versus the suit and ties of corporate America. Apple had attitude.

The two friends eventually fell out, with Wozniak leaving the company to become a teacher, but Jobs went on to launch the Apple Macintosh, with which he hoped to conquer the computer world. The crown went instead to Bill Gates, whose Microsoft persuaded 80 percent of computer buyers to use its operating system, MS-DOS, rather than buy Apple.

Many industry commentators still believe that Apple could have been sitting where Microsoft is today. That battle is over, but whether Bill Gates won it or Steve Jobs blew it remains an open question. Observers agree that an important mistake Apple made was refusing to license its operating system to other computer manufacturers. This left the door open for Microsoft's MS-DOS alternative.

After its early triumphs (the revolutionary nature of which cannot be underestimated), a series of false starts, missed opportunities, and product flops caused Apple's market share to dwindle, despite the enduring appeal of the Apple name and a high level of brand loyalty among Apple owners.

One newspaper described Jobs as a "corporate Huckleberry Finn" (begging the question, Who was the corporate Tom Sawyer?), and said his early business exploits had already made him part of American folk history. The fairy-tale story came to a sticky end in 1985 when former Pepsi chairman John Sculley, who had been brought in to add some corporate know-how to the wilting Apple, removed Jobs.

Sculley himself was booted out in 1993, after a disastrous period in which Apple's market share plummeted from 20 percent to just 8 percent. He was replaced by Michael Spindler, who lasted until 1996, by which time market share had fallen to just 5 percent. Apple was staring oblivion in the face as its long-term devotees began to switch to the Microsoft-powered PCs.

Spindler was shown the door, and Gil Amelio stepped into the hot seat. After 500 days in the post, Apple's market share had fallen to 4 percent and Amelio invited Jobs to come in and help. With two being a crowd, Amelio soon made his exit and got down to the real business of writing a book about his experiences.

After a 13-year exile, Jobs was back. The iconoclast who founded the computer company with attitude was now its only hope of survival. The wheel had come full circle. The world has changed in the intervening period, but the Apple brand and the style of its famous founder remain well matched.

THE GREATEST LESSONS

Upstarts can win.   Jobs and Wozniak seized the opportunity and changed the world through a combination of chutzpah, good fortune, and technical and marketing brilliance.

Style is all.   With the iMac, Apple may have rediscovered its inventive originality. The iMac, a vision in translucent blue, sold 278,000 units in the first six weeks, an achievement that *Fortune* magazine described as "one of the hottest computer launches ever." The iMac and Jobs' return helped Apple's share price double in less than a year.

Manage the future.   Brilliant and brilliantly successful, Apple was too busy delivering products to figure out what might happen in the future. Its personnel record is disastrously bad. Squabbles continue over who is the architect of its (perhaps brief) renaissance. The spurned CEO, Gil Amelio, claims that Jobs stepped in at just the right time, and that he, Amelio, took on a moribund company and turned it around. Amelio's angle is that he bequeathed a reenergized Apple, with $1.5 billion in the bank and a number of stunning new product lines, including the iMac.

Great Decision #3

Henry Ford's decision to start his own company in 1903 led to the first mass production line, created a mass market in automobiles, launched a corporate giant, changed perceptions of travel, led to the establishing of a variety of other industries, and provided a blueprint for industrial production.

Henry Ford's decision to mass produce was one of the most frequently cited management decisions during my research. It is difficult to argue that any other decision had such phenomenal repercussions.

First, the story. Henry Ford (1863–1947) was originally a boy racer. After spending time as a machinist's apprentice, a watch repairer, and a mechanic, he built his first car in 1896. He quickly became convinced of the commercial potential and started his own company in 1903. (There was nothing unusual in this; between 1900 and 1908 more than 500 American companies were set up to make cars.) Ford's first car was the Model A. After a year, he was selling 600 a month. In 1908, Ford's Model T was born. Through innovative use of new mass production techniques, Ford produced 15 million Model Ts between 1908 and 1927. At that time, Ford's factory at Highland Park, Michigan was the biggest in the world; more than 14,000 people worked on the 57-acre site. And it was to the world that Ford looked. He was quick to establish international operations. Ford's first overseas sales branch was opened in France in 1908 and, in 1911, Ford began making cars in the U.K.

In 1919 Ford resigned as the company's president and his son, Edsel, took over. By then the Ford company was making a car a minute. In 1923, annual sales peaked at 2,120,898. At the time, Ford's market share was in excess of 57 percent.

Ford's fans were drawn from all walks of life. In 1934 Clyde Barrow, the infamous bank robber, wrote to Ford:

Dear Sir,

While I still have got breath in my lungs I will tell you what a dandy car you make. I have drove Fords exclusively when I could get away with one. For sustained speed and freedom from trouble the Ford has got every other car skinned and even if my business hasent been strickly legal it don't hurt anything to tell you what a fine car you got in the V-8.

Yours truly,

Clyde Champion Barrow

Henry Ford developed mass production not because he blindly believed in the most advanced production methods. He was no clone of scientific management originator Frederick Taylor. (In fact, the unique Ford was no clone of anyone.) Ford believed in mass production because it meant he could make cars that people could afford. That, with staggering success, is what he achieved. At one point the company had cash reserves of $1 billion. (This did not stop Ford from maintaining, "A business that makes nothing but money is a poor kind of business.")

Ford's masterstroke was the realization that the mass car market existed; it only remained for him to provide the products the market wanted. Model Ts were black, straightforward, and affordable. The corollary of this was to prove Ford's nemesis. Reasonably priced cars demanded mass production methods. Costs could only be lowered through increased efficiency and standardization, so that more cars could be produced. Ford followed this strategy through with characteristic thoroughness. General Motors chief Alfred Sloan noted: "Mr. Ford's assembly-line automobile production, high minimum wage, and low-priced car were revolutionary and stand among the greatest contributions to our industrial culture. His basic conception of one car in one utility model at an ever lower price was what the market, especially the farm market, needed at the time."

Ford was an eccentric genius whose timing was impeccable. He was not the most likeable person in history, but he was capable of business brilliance. In May 1927, when the 15-millionth Model T was produced, Ford closed the production line. The Model T was dead, but the trouble was no one knew what was coming next. Silence reigned. Tension mounted. Finally, in November, Ford announced the arrival of the Model A, which was first sold in December 1927. Within six weeks there were 750,000 orders. As acts of marketing bravado go, Ford's dramatic closure of the Model T line and the six-month interregnum before the launch of the new model are difficult to match.

THE GREATEST LESSONS

Create your vision.   In 1907, Ford professed that his aim was to ... "build a motor car for the great multitude ... It will be so low in price that no man making a good salary will be unable to own one, and enjoy with his family the blessing of hours of pleasure in God's great open spaces ... . Everybody will be able to afford one, and everyone will have one. The horse will have disappeared from our highways, the automobile will be taken for granted." Ford's commitment to lowering prices cannot be doubted. Between 1908 and 1916 he reduced prices by 58 percent—at a time when demand was such that he could easily have raised prices. What made him do so? The drive to achieve his vision.

Inflexibility is corporate suicide.   Ford stuck rigidly to his policy of mass production and limited choice. Having given the market what it wanted, he presumed that more of the same was also what it required. He was reputed to have kicked a slightly modified Model T to pieces, such was his commitment to the unadulterated version. When other manufacturers added extras, Ford kept it simple and dramatically lost ground. The company's reliance on the Model T nearly drove it to self-destruction.

The reasons were explained by Ted Levitt in his article, "Marketing Myopia," in which he reevaluated Ford from a marketing perspective. "Mass production industries are impelled by a great drive to produce all they can. The prospect of steeply declining unit costs as output rises is more than most companies can usually resist. The profit possibilities look spectacular. All effort focuses on production. The result is that marketing gets neglected," Levitt wrote. Finally, there is overconcentration on the product, because the product lends itself to measurement and analysis.

Great Decision #4

After failing to convince Montgomery Ward to move into retailing, Robert E. Wood was hired by Sears, Roebuck in 1924. Sears chief Julius Rosenwald liked Wood's idea of retailing; Sears opened its first retail store in 1925 and became the world's largest general merchandiser.

Julius Rosenwald brought business vigor to the fledgling Sears, Roebuck. Until his arrival it had been run with entrepreneurial enthusiasm and little else. Rosenwald moved Sears forward. In 1906 Sears Roebuck opened its Chicago mail-order plant. It was the largest business building in the world, with three million square feet of floor space. Size, however, was not necessarily equated with efficiency. The Sears business was sprawling and inefficient. Customers sometimes received five articles when they wanted one, or received none at all. The logistics were a nightmare.

The company got its act together. (This in itself was a decisive move.) A time schedule was introduced so that once orders were received, they had to be dispatched within a certain amount of time. An array of belts and chutes linked arrivals and departures. Henry Ford was reputedly inspired to introduce his mass production methods after seeing them at work in the Sears Roebuck warehouse.

The next challenge for the company was to deal with growing competition from retail chains that was hurting Sears' catalog sales. The move from the country to the city was now underway; by 1920 America's urban population outnumbered its rural population for the first time. Clearly, this had a substantial effect on Sears' core market.

Robert E. Wood (1879–1969) was hired by Sears Roebuck in 1924. While Wood's interest in developing retail stores had fallen on deaf ears at Montgomery Ward, Julius Rosenwald liked the idea. He backed Wood. Sears opened its first retail store in 1925 and became the world's largest general merchandiser. By 1928 Sears had 192 retail stores. A heady pace of expansion was maintained. During one single year in the 1920s a new Sears store opened every other business day. By 1931, the retail stores formed the bulk of the company's business.

The rest of the company's history has been less distinguished. Empires disappear in commerce as surely as they do elsewhere. Even so, Sears remains a formidable retail force, with 833 department stores, over

1,300 other stores, and an array of products sold through independently owned stores.

THE GREATEST LESSONS

Hire from the competition.   Rosenwald recognized a bright idea and a bright person when he saw them. He wanted Wood on his side.

Move on.   Sears could easily have remained a rural catalog company. Richard Sears' decision to bring in Rosenwald was a good one. Rosenwald moved the company on from its initial successes. Unfortunately, the heady pace of the company's expansion and invention could not be sustained.

Great Decision #5

In 1850 Julius Reuter used carrier pigeons to communicate share prices between the end of the Belgian telegraph line in Brussels and the end of the German line in Aachen. It was the beginning of a news and information business.

In 1850, Julius Reuter (1816–99) set up a business to bridge the 76-mile gap in the telegraph wire between Belgium and Germany. It really was a gap in the market. Reuter built a company on one simple realization: that customers would be prepared to pay for information that was timely and accurate. He used carrier pigeons to forward stock market and commodity prices from Brussels, where the Belgian telegraph line ended, to Aachen, where the German line began.

On the early receipt of critical information, fortunes could be made and lost in the stock markets and bourses of Europe. Those whose money was at stake had to be sure the information was accurate. They were prepared to pay handsomely for early news from a reputable source, even if the source was a pigeon. Reuter's industry-shaping deal was actually with Heinrich Geller, who was a brewer, baker, and pigeon-fancier among other things. Geller initially undertook to deliver 45 trained pigeons. Later Geller pressed all his pigeons—200 in total—into service with Reuter.

Every day the pigeons were dispatched by train to Brussels. The next day at dawn, the pigeons began their flights home with messages secured under their wings. (Each message was secured to three birds to ensure delivery.) When they landed at Geller's home in Aachen, the messages were passed quickly on to the Reuter's office so that the information could be relayed to German destinations.

Later, when the telegraph gap was smaller, Reuter used horses rather than pigeons to carry messages. The telegraph gap was completely closed on April 16, 1851; Reuter's brilliantly conceived temporary monopoly was shut down.

Undeterred, Reuter moved to London, the financial center of the Victorian world. News, Reuters grasped, was a valuable commodity. In London he launched his famous telegraph agency. By the end of the 1850s he had succeeded in establishing a standard for news gathering and distribution. Reuter set out to be "first with the news." Above speed he placed accuracy, and alongside accuracy he set impartiality of distribution. Achieving objectivity in reporting is difficult, but Reuters earned an enviable reputation for doing just that. Today, the strength of the Reuters name is based on the core values that its founder inculcated in the company.

Reuter began carrying news reports of events on the mainland of Europe to leading British newspapers. Eventually, he persuaded even the *London Times* to publish his reports. This presented him with an opportunity to build his brand. For the first time, Reuter's name appeared as the source under news reports. The move marked a milestone in the branding of information.

An early scoop involved Reuter's transmitting a summary of an important speech by the King of Sardinia that had important implications for the unification of Italy. His remarks were read in England the same day. The report from the *Times'* own correspondent didn't appear until four days later. (Another scoop wrongly attributed to Reuter involved a speech by Napoleon III a few days earlier; on that occasion, however, the news agency was beaten by the *Times.*)

For a century, Reuters was particularly the news agency of the British Empire. This allowed the company to grow rapidly throughout the first half of the twentieth century. As Britain's imperial power waned, Reuters moved into selling economic information to the world's trading community. This generated annual pretax profits of $420 million by the end of the 1980s.

Julius Reuter died in 1899. The humorous magazine, *Punch,* mourned his passing:

> *They need full epitaph, whose fame*
> *Were else oblivion's easy prey;*
> *'Tis here unneeded, when each day*
> *A myriad prints bear Reuter's name.*

THE GREATEST LESSONS

Information is power.   And timely information is even more powerful. Reuter's simple realization remains true to this day. Ask Michael

Bloomberg. His media and communications empire is built on the same realization.

Opportunities abound.   Julius Reuter was first and foremost an entrepreneur. In another age, at another time, he would have made his fortune by identifying another opportunity.

Time is of the essence.   Julius Reuter may not have been the first to say "The quicker, the better," but he would have sympathized with the sentiment.

Temporary monopolies are the goal of any business.   Business heaven is a monopoly. In reality, temporary monopolies tend not to last very long. (And, while they exist, it is better not to draw too much attention to them, or to refer to them as "monopolies.")

Great Decision #6

By the late 1970s, the once great Swiss watch industry was on its knees. Then, with a last throw of the dice, Swiss manufacturers decided to work together to come up with a make-or-break response to cheap competition. The result was Swatch. Almost overnight, the dormant Swiss watch industry was revived. The humble timepiece became a fashion accessory and the Swiss share of the worldwide watch market rose from 15 percent to over 50 percent.

The Swatch story is a classic tale of triumph over adversity. Between the mid-1970s and 1983, the Swiss watchmaking industry saw its share of the world watch market decimated, from 30 percent to just 9 percent, a loss of two-thirds in less than ten years. As Japanese watches swept all before them, the Swiss were losing out even in their traditional stronghold in quality timepieces. The writing was on the wall for what were once regarded as the finest watchmakers in the world.

Then rescue came at the last gasp. Leading Swiss manufacturers decided to join together in a consortium called ASUAG-SSIH. This was later reformed with the help of businessman Nicolas Hayek (born 1928) as SMH—the Swiss Corporation for the Microelectronics and Watchmaking Industries. Ultimately it became the Swatch Group. The group thought it would be better to go down together, with all guns blazing, than to timidly surrender in isolation, watching the market crumble away.

It was Ernst Thomke, president of ETA SA, and ETA's chief engineer, Jacques Muller, who came up with the winning idea. Thomke had developed the Delirium, then the slimmest watch in the world. He suggested a low-cost version of the Delirium to combat the Japanese threat. It was Thomke who developed the technical specifications of the original Swatch, as well as the all-important marketing concept.

The creation of the first Swatch was fraught with problems. For one thing, Thomke had to secretly buy the patent rights to manufacture key components of his daring creation. Another problem was that traditional manufacturing facilities in Switzerland were forbidden to produce coils or work with plastics.

Research and development were carried out in secret. Nicolas Hayek, acting as adviser to the watch industry, supported the project and played a key role in making sure that production stayed in Switzerland. Hayek became chairman and CEO of the Swatch Group in 1986, after it was created out of the merger of the ASUAG and SSIH watch companies. The Group, which also markets the brands Blancpain, Omega, Longines, Rado, Tissot, Certina, Mido, Hamilton, Balmain, Calvin Klein, Flik Flak, and Lanco, has its headquarters in Biel-Bienne. (Thomke left Swatch in 1992 after a falling out with Hayek, and became the Swiss turnaround expert.)

The first attempt to pilot the new product in America in 1982 was a dismal failure. It was only when the product was advertised as the "second watch" under the slogan, "You have a second home, why not a second watch?" that it became a hit with consumers.

The name was shortened to the "S" watch and then to Swatch. The Swatch was based on the simple premise that the watch could become a disposable or replaceable fashion item.

As a result, the Swatch was simple. The first model had fewer than 51 parts, far fewer than any other analog quartz watch. A traditional mechanical watch, by contrast, had more than 125 parts. Technical simplicity was offset by bright colors and ever-changing styles and variations. The people behind the upstart watches gambled that consumers couldn't care less about the number of parts, but would respond to the novelty of a profusion of Swatch styles.

The pace with which new designs and new technology are introduced has always been the key to keeping the Swatch brand fresh. In recent years, for example, new developments have taken place alongside the standard plastic Swatch. New models have been introduced, including the Chrono and the Irony (a metal watch, which provides an ironic twist to the Swatch concept).

Other novelty innovations include the light-powered Swatch Solar; the melodic alarm of the Swatch MusiCall; and the world's first watch with a built-in pager, called the Beep Swatch. Another typical Swatch innovation is the Access, with a built-in access control function that can be used as a ski pass at many of the world's ski resorts. Perhaps the most interesting development from Swatch is its link-up with Mercedes for the production of a miniature car.

THE GREATEST LESSONS

Reinvent old products to create new markets.   The Swatch was made not by Swiss craftspeople but by robots. Manufacturing costs were low. Swatches were sealed into plastic cases. Repair was not an option. Unlike earlier Swiss watches, the Swatch was not meant to be handed down from one generation to another; rather it was the ultimate in disposable timepieces. Consumers were invited to throw away their old Swatches and buy new ones. The key to the brand positioning was the fresh appeal of a constant supply of new designs. For the first time, watches changed with the season.

Design conquers all.   In an industry characterized by conservative values, the Swatch was different, cool and fun. The secret to keeping the brand strong was constant innovation. New designs and colors, changing every six months at first and then more frequently, assured return buyers. Keen pricing—they sold for between $25 and $35—assured they were affordable for young people. It's a formula that's been working ever since. By 1997, more than 200 million units had been sold. Swatch is now operating in 72 markets worldwide.

Great Decision #7

In 1981 Bill Gates decided to license MS-DOS to IBM while IBM ceded control of the license for all non-IBM PCs. This laid the foundation for Microsoft's huge success and IBM's fall from grace.

We've all tried it. We've all bluffed, giving the impression that we're in a much better bargaining position than we actually are. Perhaps that's what was running through Bill Gates' mind when he changed the face of the computing industry.

The story revolves around the insight, vision, and opportunism of Gates and his partner Paul Allen, and the laggardly behavior of IBM. Despite being the dominant computer firm on planet earth, IBM was late off the mark with the PC. The company that dominated the mainframe computer business failed to recognize the importance of—and the threat presented by—the rise of the personal computer. By the time Big Blue decided to enter the PC market in 1980, Apple, which had pioneered the desktop computer, had become a $100 million business.

Frank Cary, IBM chairman at the time, ordered his people to produce an IBM-badged PC by August 1981. Already in catch-up mode, the IBMers put in charge of the project made two fundamental technical errors. Both mistakes came from a single decision to go outside the company for the two critical elements of the new machine—the microprocessor that would be at the heart of the new PC and the operating system. Intel agreed to supply the chips, and a small, relatively unknown software company based in Seattle agreed to supply the operating system.

Executives from Big Blue thought they were simply saving time by outsourcing a non-core activity to a small contractor. After all, they were in the computer hardware business, where the real money and power lay. Without an IBM box, the Microsoft brand was meaningless. At least, that's what IBM thought.

What IBM couldn't see, Gates saw very clearly. The world of computing was on the brink of a major change, what the management theorists like to call a paradigm change. Gates understood in a way that the old IBM guard could not that software, not hardware, was the key to the future. He knew, too, that the muscle of IBM, the market leader, would be required to establish a common standard, or platform, for software applications. That platform would be Q-DOS—an existing operating system that Gates bought for $50,000 from another company and that was renamed MS-DOS by Microsoft. But even Gates could not have imagined just how lucrative the deal would be for Microsoft.

Bill Gates was too bright not to realize that if he played his cards right, his operating system, MS-DOS, could become the industry standard. At that time, the operating system was just one of several on the market.

Many inside the computer industry felt at that time that from a purely technical perspective, MS-DOS had some serious drawbacks. Apple was already established as the provider of choice for desktop computers. Apple's founders had brought a new attitude and culture to the computer business. The Apple brand was way ahead of Microsoft, in terms of both image and perceived quality. Apple's machines were popular because they were simpler to operate and fun to use. The company had yet to develop the famous icon-based Apple Macintosh operating system, but the signs were already there that the people at Apple were ahead of the game.

The launch of the IBM PC was initially a commercial success. But the company ended up giving away most of the profits from its PC business to its two partners. Under the initial contract between IBM and Microsoft, Big Blue agreed to fund most of the development costs of MS-DOS, but only Microsoft was allowed to license the system to third parties. This was the killer clause. Microsoft's decision to go for a license was an act of bravado and brilliance; among the people canvassed for this book it was the most often mentioned great decision.

As the PC industry exploded, thousands of new competitors entered the market. Virtually all of them ended up using MS-DOS and paying Microsoft for the privilege. But IBM's mistakes didn't end there. When it recognized its initial error, IBM failed to renegotiate the licensing contract or to break with Microsoft. Even more mystifying, senior managers at IBM killed an internally developed operating system that could have broken Microsoft's stranglehold on the PC market.

More than a decade later, IBM was still manufacturing more PCs than any other company, but its personal systems division was losing money. The only companies making large profits in the highly competitive PC business were the suppliers of the microchips and operating systems. To this day, the computing industry is dominated by two brands: Intel and Microsoft.

THE GREATEST LESSONS

Vision overcomes.   Since the early days of Microsoft, Gates has pursued his vision of "a computer on every desk and in every home." (Interestingly, the original slogan was "A computer on every desk in every home, running Microsoft software"; the last part is often left off these days because it makes some people uncomfortable).

Look to the future; then invent it.   Looking back now, the spread of personal computers from the office into the home seems almost inevitable. Hindsight is a wonderful thing. Foresight, however, is much more lucrative, as Gates has shown. It is important to remember, too, that the ubiquitous screens and keyboards we all take for granted today were the stuff of science fiction just a couple of decades ago. Back in the 1960s when futurists in America tried to predict the trends that were likely to shape society in the rest of the century, they completely missed the rise of the PC.

It is not true that Bill Gates alone was responsible for putting the PC in homes and offices all over the world, any more than Henry Ford was responsible for the rise of the automobile. What the two had in common, however, was the vision to see what was possible and the willingness to make that vision a reality.

Gates set about achieving his vision by transforming Microsoft into a major player in the computer industry and using its dominant position to create a platform for the huge growth in applications. What Gates realized very early on was that in order for his vision to succeed, it was essential that an industry standard be created. He knew too that whoever got there first would have a major opportunity to become the leader in the computing industry.

Make your own luck.   Microsoft clinched the deal to supply the operating system for IBM. Gates was lucky. Had the same opportunity fallen to one of his Silicon Valley peers, the outcome might have been very different. In Bill Gates, IBM had picked the one man who would not fumble the ball. On such moments does history turn. (It could be said that though MS-DOS was a cash cow, Microsoft's real leap forward came with the launch of Windows 3.)

If you're small, find someone who isn't and make friends. Ironically, it was the muscle of the IBM brand behind the operating system that gave the Microsoft brand its power. Big Blue had dominated the mainframe business for years and, somewhat belatedly, was preparing to enter the PC market. The credibility of the IBM name would be crucial in the battle ahead. Gates judged correctly that the best opportunity for establishing an industry standard other than one based around the Apple system was to be connected with the arrival in the PC market of the world's most trusted computer manufacturer. For many years, IBM's proud boast was that "No one ever got fired for buying an IBM." At that time, it had a reputation for dependability unmatched in the computer world. The IBM PC was bound to take a big slice of the market for desktop computers.

The fact that IBM-badged machines were about to flood the market also meant that the operating system IBM used would be catapulted into first or second place. Every single PC shipped by IBM would have MS-DOS installed. For Microsoft it was the perfect Trojan horse. Every IBM-badged PC that landed on a desk gave a free ride to the Microsoft operating system that lay hidden inside. This was Bill Gates' amazing piece of luck. What happened afterward goes a long way in explaining why Bill Gates, and not Steve Jobs or some other Silicon Valley entrepreneur, is now the richest man in the computer world.

Great Decision #8

In the late 1960s, a New York ice cream maker named Reuben Mattus decided that the future for his business lay in selling ice cream all year round to supermarkets. He came up with a new brand targeted at this market. It worked. Luxury, premium-priced, sexy ice cream was born.

Reuben Mattus arrived in the United States from Poland in 1921. He was eight and, was accompanied by his widowed mother. To make money, Mattus' mother sold lemon ices made from lemons squeezed by hand.

Mattus was a youthful entrepreneur. In 1932, he set up Senator Frozen Products in the Bronx and, by the late 1950s, had built it up into a successful firm that sold, among other things, an ice cream called Ciro's through outlets such as drug and grocery stores. By the 1960s, Mattus could see that the future belonged to larger outlets. He wanted to distribute ice cream through the supermarkets that were springing up. With their superior refrigeration and wide appeal, he believed the bigger retail outlets offered a market for ice cream all year round.

However, his Ciro's brand was soon squeezed out by the large dairies that picked up on the idea and offered the large retail chains incentive deals that Ciro's couldn't match.

Mattus wasn't so easily put off. He came up with another idea: a luxury brand of ice cream made from fresh cream, real fruit, and natural ingredients and marketed through the use of imaginatively named flavors. Somewhat bizarrely, a Danish-sounding name, he decided, was the perfect touch to differentiate his new brand from the competition.

The first three Haagen-Dazs flavors were basic—vanilla, chocolate, and coffee—and were sold through New York delicatessens. The response was immediate and positive. Within a few weeks other stores across America were placing orders for the new ice cream. Such was its success that by the 1970s, sales of the new brand had eclipsed those of Ciro's, which was closed down.

Throughout the early 1970s, Haagen-Dazs sales increased even though the product had no formal advertising and only word-of-mouth endorsements. Remarkably, this was sufficient to increase product distribution to urban centers and college towns in the Northeast. People began to write from across the country asking how they could get Haagen-Dazs in their area. A few fanatics even volunteered to distribute the product themselves.

What happened next was a defining moment for the brand. It took the product from being simply an ice cream brand and made it a retail phenomenon in its own right. Mattus' daughter came up with the idea of a dipping store, an entire retail outlet devoted solely to the Haagen-Dazs brand. The first store was opened in Brooklyn and ushered in a new era for the brand. It was followed by more stores in cities across the United States.

By 1982, the company was pushing into new markets. Expansion into Canada was a natural next step. This was followed by a partnership with a leading Japanese dairy, and by the end of the 1980s, the ice cream had crossed the Atlantic to the Old World, where Europeans greeted the sensuous advertising that announced its arrival with enthusiasm.

The mid-1980s were kind to Haagen-Dazs. It's appeal to the "me generation" was direct. The passion for self-indulgence was all-consuming, and consumed it was by the truckload. By the early 1990s, Haagen-Dazs had become the coolest new bedroom accessory on the market. Ads featuring beautiful semi-naked men and women dipping into the luxurious ice cream cartons adorned the pages of magazines and newspapers and appeared on billboards. Meanwhile, behind the scenes, control shifted.

The 1980s also marked the arrival of another luxury ice cream brand: Ben & Jerry's Homemade. The story of the company founded by Ben Cohen and Jerry Greenfield in an abandoned Vermont gas station is well known. Their alternative ice cream empire competes directly with Haagen-Dazs. (The other great decision in the ice cream business came in 1977 when Ben & Jerry decided to take a $5 correspondence course in ice cream making. They now make a lot more ice cream than they ever thought possible.)

What Ben & Jerry's brought to the market was luxury ice cream with hippie attitudes. In some respects, it was the natural next thing. After the pure hedonism of the 1980s, the baby boomer generation was attracted to frozen desserts with a moral message. Calorie concerns could wait, the new ice cream addicts felt, but saving the world couldn't. The combination of Ben & Jerry's fat-full fudge sundaes with utopian business values on top was seductive. Their hippie humor—with flavors named like Cherry Garcia, inspired by the leader of the Grateful Dead—also appealed. They squeezed into the market Haagen-Dazs invented.

THE GREATEST LESSONS

Start young.   Mattus was an upstart entrepreneur who learned as he went along.

Aim high.   As he contemplated the possibilities, Mattus could have gone for the lower end of the market. Instead, he opted for the premium-priced top end—a much harder choice, but one that reaped impressive results.

Strategize.   Strategy does work. The development of Haagen-Dazs is one of those helpful examples that prove strategizing can and does work. Mattus weighed the situation and chose his strategy. Of course, the usual helping of luck and happenstance was then required to make the strategy work. (It also helps when your children come up with bright ideas.)

THE NAME GAME

In business, names matter. "When we came up with the name Virgin instead of Slipped Disc Records for our record company in the winter of 1969, I had some vague idea of the name being catchy and applying to lots of other products for young people," recalls Virgin chief Richard Branson. "It would have been interesting to have tracked the success of the Virgin companies or otherwise if we had called the company Slipped Disc Records. Slipped Disc Condoms might not have worked as well."[1]

In 1936, Kiichiro Toyoda was contemplating the future of the company his father had founded. He visited the United States and Europe and decided the future was in car making. A new direction required a new name, so he launched a competition to find a name. In 1936 the company was renamed Toyota—a subtle change, admittedly, that in Japanese characters conveys speed and uses eight strokes, a number suggesting prosperity. From the Western perspective, Toyota is pronounceable and attractively meaningless.

If you go back into the mists of corporate time, there is Harley Procter of Procter & Gamble fame, reading his Bible in church and being struck by the phrase "out of ivory palaces"—and finding just the name for a soap.

Mere semantics? I think not. The first selection of great decisions in this category proves the point. IBM, Walt Disney, and McKinsey & Co. provide stellar examples. They got it right: Names matter.

Great Decision #9

In 1924 Thomas Watson Sr. changed the name of the Computing Tabulating Recording Company to International Business Machines. The company had no international operations, but it was a bold statement of ambitions.

Thomas Watson, Senior (1874–1956) was the creator of the corporate colossus that became IBM, "Big Blue." Watson turned IBM from nothing into the stuff of corporate and stock market legends, a company that continues to flourish long after Watson's death. Indomitable, perhaps unforgiving, Watson molded the company into what he wanted it to be through the very force of his own personality, experience, and convictions. Watson was relentless in his quest to create a substantial organization.

The beginnings were not auspicious. Watson joined the Computing Tabulating Recording Company in 1914. Under Watson the company's revenues doubled from $4.2 million to $8.3 million by 1917. Initially making everything from butcher's scales to meat slicers, the company's activities gradually began to concentrate on tabulating machines that processed information mechanically on punched cards.

When Watson boldly renamed the company International Business Machines he was overstating the company's credentials. It was not an international company (though IBM Japan was established before the Second World War). It was not even a particularly large company.

The brilliance of the name was in its ambition and its pithy summary of the business the company was in. This second point sounds obvious, but "business machines" was a prescient phrase. It encompassed computers and the high-tech products made by the company today as it did the basic products made at the time.

IBM became the archetypal modern corporation and its managers the ultimate role models, with their regulation somber suits, white shirts, plain ties, zeal for selling, and company song. Behind the stereotype lay a belief in competing vigorously and providing quality service. Later, competitors would complain that IBM's sheer size won it orders. This was only partly true. IBM's size masked a deep commitment to managing customer accounts, providing service, and building relationships.

IBM's development was helped by the 1937 Wages and Hours Act, which required U.S. companies to record employees' hours worked and wages paid. The existing machines couldn't cope with the task and Watson instigated work on a solution. In 1944 the Mark 1 was launched, followed by the Selective Sequence Electronic Calculator in 1947. By then IBM's revenues were $119 million and the company was set to make the great leap forward to become the world's largest computer company and one of the world's most valuable brands.

Watson was succeeded by his son, Thomas Watson Jr. "The secret I learned early on from my father was to run scared and never think I had made it," said the younger Watson. Under Thomas Watson Sr. there was never any danger of his son or the company as a whole becoming complacent.

THE GREATEST LESSONS

Think big.   American Business Machines might have caught on, but the name International Business Machines had a panache and ambition that played no small part in shaping the company's culture and helping it to grow.

Think international.   There is nothing to suggest that Thomas Watson was anything other than a typical businessman of the early twentieth century. He did not travel a huge amount. (He did speak five languages.) But he recognized the global potential. He thought internationally, even though he was no internationalist.

Great Decision #10

Walt Disney listened to his wife, Lillian, and decided to call his cartoon mouse Mickey rather than Mortimer. Entertainment was never the same after Mickey and Minnie debuted in Steamboat Willie *in 1928.*

"I hope we never lose sight of one fact—that this was all started by a mouse," Walt Disney was fond of saying in his later years.[2] The origins of Disney's mousey inspiration are recounted with many variations. At one time it was reputed that early in his career Disney befriended a family of mice in his office. Their regular appearances on his drawing board proved inspirational. Nice story.

Alternatively, the *Daily Sketch* reported in 1938 that, "On his way back to Hollywood in an upper berth he could not sleep. The continuous but slight creaking of the woodwork in his compartment sounded like a million mice in conference. The idea made him laugh and in that split second Mickey Mouse was born." Perhaps.

The facts are that the mouse in question began life as Mortimer Mouse. Walt Disney's wife, Lilly, did not take to the name and suggested Mickey as a replacement. Walt listened. Whether this was to placate his wife or out of some deep realization that Mickey was the ideal name to launch a business empire will never be known. (Of course, why Mickey works and Mortimer doesn't is a matter of serious debate. "Maybe Mickey Mouse didn't sound quite as onomatopoeic as Mortimer Mouse, but was a friendlier, more informal name, suggesting an affinity with the common man," observed one book with due solemnity.[3])

On Sunday, November 18, 1928, Mickey Mouse was featured in one of the only cinematic epics of seven minutes in length: *Steamboat Willie.* This was the first cartoon that synchronized sound and action. *Steamboat Willie* reversed the tide of Walt Disney's fortunes. "A peach of a synchronization job all the way, bright, snappy, and fitting the situation perfectly," said *Variety.* "Kept the audience laughing and chuckling," said *Weekly Film Review.*

Walt Disney was thankful for every chuckle, because up to that point his career had been decidedly patchy. Chicago-born Walter E. Disney (1901–1966) grew up on a farm in Missouri before returning to Chicago to study art. In 1920, Disney moved to Kansas City, where he worked for the animator Ub Iwerks. Along the way, Disney also went bankrupt, with debts of $15,000 following the failure of his Laugh O Gram Company of Kansas City. In 1923 he left Kansas City for Los Angeles in search of a job in the movie business. He wasn't the first and he certainly wasn't the last. Initially, Disney was singularly unsuccessful. No job materialized. Disney thought he might have missed the boat entirely.

Disney could have returned to Kansas. He didn't. Instead, he rented a camera, assembled an animation stand, and set up a studio in his uncle's garage. In 1923, the 21-year-old Walt Disney was in business with his older brother Roy. In 1923, Disney, the corporation, was born.

Disney got off to a decidedly poor start. Its first film, *Alice,* barely kept the company going. The second, *Oswald the Rabbit,* was released in 1927. Walt's business acumen temporarily deserted him and he lost control of the film rights. Then his luck changed: The mouse materialized and he listened to his wife.

Walt Disney later recalled the moment of creation: "Out of the trouble and confusion stood a mocking, merry little figure. Vague and indefinable at first. But it grew and grew. And finally arrived—a mouse. A romping rollicking little mouse. The idea completely engulfed me."[4]

After Mickey's invention, Disney never looked back. *Flowers & Trees* (1932) brought the world Technicolor. By 1937, Disney was producing the feature-length *Snow White and the Seven Dwarfs.* More followed, including *Pinocchio* (1940), *Fantasia* (1940), *Dumbo* (1941), and *Bambi* (1942). After the Second World War, Disney introduced his cartoon characters to real actors in classics including *Treasure Island* (1950), *Davy Crockett* (1955), and *Mary Poppins* (1964). The effect was continued huge success for Disney. This bred even greater ambitions. In 1955, Disney opened Disneyland in Anaheim, California. Disney World in Orlando, Florida opened in 1971. Then the Magic Kingdom became mired in corporate reality until it turned the corner with the 1987 blockbusters—*Three Men and a Baby; Good Morning, Vietnam; Beauty and the Beast;* and *The Lion King.* Eurodisney and Disney's Michael Eisner are successes in keeping with Walt's blueprint.

THE GREATEST LESSONS

Listen and you shall find. Not even an epochal character like Walt Disney had all the answers. Listening is one of the great unrecognized skills of business leadership.

Persist, and then persist some more. "He was at least halfway convinced that he was too late, by perhaps six years, to break into animation, but [it] was the only area in which he had any prior experience," noted one of Disney's later biographers.[5] The Disney Corporation didn't happen overnight, and was probably all the better for that. Walt Disney persisted. He believed and he recruited fellow believers.

Great Decision #11

After the death of the company founder, the two offices of consulting firm McKinsey & Co. went their separate ways in 1939. A.T. Kearney launched his own firm in Chicago. Marvin Bower, in New York, kept the McKinsey name. He decided, correctly, that using his name would only lead clients to expect his involvement in every assignment. McKinsey became The Firm in the consulting industry.

Insiders in the consultancy McKinsey & Company always call it *The Firm*. There is an assumption that when it comes to management consultancy, McKinsey operates on a different plane—where the bills are larger, the hours longer, the standards higher, the results better, and the people brighter. McKinsey consultants like to think of themselves as the movie stars of the business world. They dazzle you not with their expensive coiffures, but with their intellects.

The Firm is more than a mere consultancy. It has its own ethos: Staid suits and high standards. Clean-cut and conservative. It is obsessively professional and hugely successful; a slick, well-oiled financial machine. McKinsey is one of the great brands of the professional service industry.

Tributes to McKinsey are easy to find. Most examinations of the world of management consultants stop at this company's portals and pay homage. "The most well-known, most secretive, most high-priced, most prestigious, most consistently successful, most envied, most trusted, most disliked management consulting firm on earth," is how *Fortune* described McKinsey. Tom Peters prefers to observe that, "McKinsey has a stratospheric belief in itself." There is no hyperbole in Peters' observation. It is simple, and a matter of fact.

McKinsey is driven by belief, faith in the McKinsey doctrine. Self-effacing modesty is not on the agenda. Modesty and McKinsey are as comfortable with each other as the Queen of England would be with Arnold Schwarzenegger.

Apart from its somewhat overblown aspirations, what is so special about McKinsey? After all, it is not the oldest consultancy company. Arthur D. Little can trace its lineage back to the 1880s. Nor is McKinsey the biggest consultancy company in the world. Andersen Consulting dwarfs it in terms of revenues and numbers of consultants (but not, significantly, in revenue per consultant). McKinsey is special because it likes to think of itself as the best, and it has developed a self-perpetuating aura that it *is* unquestionably the best.

McKinsey's faith in its own brilliance is part of a unique corporate culture. Its creation can largely be attributed to a single man, Marvin Bower, who joined the business in the 1930s.

Marvin Bower (born 1903) joined the fledgling firm of James O. McKinsey (1889–1937) in 1933, at a time when management consulting was still called "management engineering." Bower was a Harvard-trained lawyer, originally from Cleveland. Soon after Bower's arrival, McKinsey left to run Marshall Field & Company. He died in 1937, leaving Bower in the company's New York office and A.T. Kearney in the Chicago office. In 1939 the two split, and Kearney set up a new company in his own name.

Bower did not change the name of his firm. He shrewdly decided that clients would demand his involvement in all projects if his name was up in lights. It seems a small decision. But it was also understated, self-effacing, professional, and made with an eye on the business implications.

"My vision was to provide advice on managing to top executives and to do it with the professional standards of a leading law firm," said Bower. Consequently, McKinsey consultants were "associates" who had "engagements" rather than mere jobs, and the firm was a "practice" rather than a business (proof again that semantics really do matter). "The entire ethos of McKinsey was to be very respectable, the kind of people CEOs naturally relate to. That's the enduring legacy of Marvin Bower," says former McKinsey consultant George Binney.

Throughout the 1940s and 1950s, McKinsey expanded in North America. It opened its first overseas office in London in 1959, followed by Melbourne, Amsterdam, Dusseldorf, Paris, Zurich, and Milan. In 1997, McKinsey had 74 offices in 38 countries.

Bower's gospel was that the interests of the client should come first, increasing the company's revenues second. "Unless the client could trust McKinsey, we could not work with them," said Bower. If you looked after the client, the profits would look after themselves. High charges were not a means to greater profits, according to McKinsey, but a simple and effective means of ensuring that clients took McKinsey seriously.

Bower's other rules were that consultants should keep quiet about the affairs of clients; should tell the truth and be prepared to challenge the client's opinion; and should only agree to do work that was necessary and that they could do well. To this he added a few idiosyncratic twists, such as insisting that all McKinsey consultants wear hats—except, for some reason, in the San Francisco office—and long socks.

Bower also changed the company's recruitment policy. Instead of hiring experienced executives with in-depth knowledge of a particular industry, he began recruiting graduate students who could learn how to be good problem solvers and consultants. This was a novel approach at the time, but it set a precedent and changed the emphasis in consulting from passing on a narrow range of experience, toward utilizing a wide range of analytical and problem-solving techniques.

Though the management consulting world developed a high-charging, opportunistic reputation, Bower managed to stand apart. True or not, he created an impression of hardworking, clean-living decency. Even now, once recruited, McKinsey consultants know where they stand. The firm's policy remains one of the most simple: "Seniority in McKinsey correlates directly with achievement," it says. The weak are shown the door. "If a consultant ceases to progress with the Firm or is ultimately unable to demonstrate the skills and qualities required of a principal, he or she is asked to leave McKinsey," says the company's recruitment brochure.

Bower's approach was commonsensical and free of fashionable baggage. "Business has not changed in the past sixty years. The basic way of running it is the same. There have been thousands of changes in methods but not in command and control. Many companies say they want to change but they need to empower people below. More cohesion is needed rather than hierarchy," he said in 1995.

The culture Bower created continues to thrive. The mystique of McKinsey, The Firm, is untouched. It is obsessively professional, hugely successful, and not given to false modesty. "We do not learn from clients. Their standards aren't high enough. We learn from other McKinsey partners," a McKinsey consultant once confided to *Forbes* magazine.

THE GREATEST LESSONS

The company is bigger than one person.   Bower & Co. would have tied the firm inevitably to the career of Marvin Bower. Bower realized that the business needed to be bigger than a single individual. Bower himself set an impressive example. In 1963, on reaching the age of sixty, he sold his shares back to the firm at their book value. McKinsey laid its cards on the table. It played hard, but straight. If Big Blue was the computer company to trust, McKinsey was the consulting firm to trust. McKinsey has largely managed to sustain that stature.

Set high standards.   When there was no reputable profession of management consulting, Marvin Bower created one. Professional behavior merited professional prices.

Stand for something.   Clients knew—and know—where they stand with McKinsey. Its ethos is clear, as is its modus operandi. Bower's view was that values make both the person and the business. American Express chief Harvey Golub, an ex-McKinsey consultant, labels Bower as "one of the finest leaders in American business ever," and says, "He led that firm according to a set of values, and it was the principle of using values to help shape and guide an organization that was probably the most important thing I took away."

Notes

[1]Branson, Richard, BBC "Money Programme" Lecture, 1998.

[2]Holliss, Richard and Sibley, Brian, *The Disney Studio Story*, Octopus, 1988.

[3]Holliss.

[4]Holliss.

[5]Schickel, Richard, *The Disney Version*, Simon & Schuster, New York, 1968.

MARKETING MAGIC

"While great devices are invented in the laboratory, great products are invented in the Marketing Department," says author William Davidow. This might help clear up the mystery as to what marketing actually involves. The confusion is inevitable when you are told (by Alfred Taubman), "There is more similarity in the marketing challenge of selling a precious painting by Degas and a frosted mug of root beer than you ever thought possible."

In the hands of persuasive marketers, anything is possible. Publisher P.T. Barnum decided to promote a woman who claimed to be George Washington's nurse in the late 1830s. Barnum became a master of promotion, sowing the seeds for the growth of popular entertainment as well as promotional skills.

Marketing is the essence of business. "Marketing is the distinguishing, the unique function of the business. A business is set apart from all other human organizations by the fact that it markets a product or a service," says Peter Drucker. We all sell something. It is just that some are better at selling than others.

The greatest marketing decisions are marked by their simplicity, opportunism, and success. "Good companies will meet needs; great companies will create markets," says the leading marketing thinker, Philip Kotler. "Market leadership is gained by envisioning new products, services, lifestyles, and ways to raise living standards. There is a vast difference between companies that offer me-too products and those that create new product and service values not even imagined by the marketplace. Ultimately, marketing at its best is about value creation and raising the world's living standards."[1]

Noble thoughts. The truth is that humdrum marketing decisions can change the world. "Marketing is too important to be left to the marketing department," said David Packard, cofounder of Hewlett-Packard. Marketing should be the job of everyone in an organization. The CEO has to be Chief Marketing Officer.

Great Decision #12

Richard Sears' decision to put all his products together in a catalog laid the basis for the huge success of Sears, Roebuck. It also opened up an entirely new rural market.

There was a time when markets lay undiscovered and untapped; huge opportunities lay waiting to be discovered. Those lucky enough to discover them often changed the shape of entire industries. Sears Roebuck is one example. The Sears story is basically one of the discovery of a vast new market: the rural, isolated, farming communities of the United States.

In the 1880s, the total population of the United States was 58 million, around one-fifth of the current population. The majority of people—about 65 percent—lived in the countryside. Richard Sears was one of them. He lived in the isolated outpost of North Redwood, Minnesota, where he was an agent at the Minneapolis and St. Louis railway station. Trains didn't stop often in North Redwood, so Sears traded a few things when they came his way—things like lumber and coal. One of the items that came Sears' way was a consignment of watches. These sold well, so Sears ordered some more and, in 1886, started the R.W. Sears Watch Company in Minneapolis.

Sears then moved to Chicago and recruited Alvah C. Roebuck to help him. In 1893, Sears Roebuck & Company was born. The company moved into the mail-order business, selling watches and jewelry. It published a 32-page catalog in 1891. By 1895 the catalog was 532 pages long and included everything from fishing tackle to glassware, from millinery to saddles. In 1893 sales were $400,000; in 1895, they were over $750,000.

At that point the company was a huge success, but the challenge was to take it further. In 1895, a Chicago clothing manufacturer named Julius Rosenwald bought a share in the company. It was Rosenwald who built on the lucrative foundations established by the entrepreneurial Sears and Roebuck.

Sears brought entrepreneurial energy and marketing magic to the company. One of his initiatives, for example, was a system of rewards for customers who passed copies of the catalog on to friends and relatives. This idea was tested out in Iowa. Customers received 24 copies of the catalog to distribute. If the recipients of the catalogs placed orders, the original customers received rewards.

The Sears catalog was a marketing classic. It brought the world to the isolated farms of Nebraska and the Midwest. It was a feast for the new consumers. A piano? Yours for $138 (in the 1909 catalog). One of those new-fangled cameras? Just over $100 for the Reflex Camera. Kitchen items? Try the enameled steel cooking range for $25. Fashion? Silk neckties at 29 cents. The whole world was available in the Sears catalog, and it could be delivered to the remotest of doorsteps.

THE GREATEST LESSONS

Satisfied customers are your best advertisement. Sears may not have approached business in a particularly systematic way, but he knew how to sell. The rise of Sears Roebuck is an exemplary tale of buying and selling. Sears moved from one satisfied customer base to another, using word-of-mouth recommendations and enlisting his customers as his ad agency.

Hustle, then organize. Sears was an entrepreneurial hustler; Rosenwald was the organizer. "Richard Sears gave the company his name. But it was not he who made it into a modern business enterprise," Peter Drucker recounts.[2] "Sears's own operations could hardly be called a 'business'. He was a shrewd speculator, buying up distress-merchandise and offering it, one batch at a time, through spectacular advertising. Every one of his deals was a complete transaction in itself which, when finished, liquidated itself and the business with it. But his way of operation could never found a business, let alone perpetuate it. In fact, he would have been forced out of business within a few years, as all the many people before him had been who operated on a similar basis."

Great Decision #13

In 1915 Coca-Cola decided to run a competition to design a bottle for its increasingly popular drink. One of the best known icons of the twentieth century was created free of charge, gathering enormous publicity along the way. Great decision? Just look at the brand.

Marketing tends to be ingrained in a company. Great marketing decisions rarely happen in isolation. Marketing inspiration is cultural as much as anything. One of the companies with the lengthiest and most impressive marketing pedigrees is Coca-Cola. It has sought out marketing magic from the early days of its existence.

The fabled brand was first conceived in May of 1886 in Atlanta, Georgia by a pharmacist named John Styth Pemberton. His "brain tonic" contained a leaf from a South American tree and West African seeds as well as caramel, phosphoric acid, and a combination of seven "natural flavors" that remains a well-protected secret to this day. Pemberton's bookkeeper, Frank Robinson, named the beverage Coca-Cola. Robinson also wrote the name with a slanting flourish. (A few years later, in 1894 Caleb Bradham in North Carolina began to sell a drink he had developed to help relieve dyspepsia. It contained pepsin and evolved into Pepsi-Cola. But that's another story.)

Pemberton's drink was first sold at a soda fountain in Jacob's Pharmacy in Atlanta, by Willis Venable. It sold for five cents a glass. During its first year, sales averaged six glasses a day. This generated a grand first year's income of $50.

Coca-Cola advertised and promoted itself with a flourish from the very start. John Pemberton spent $73.96 on banners and advertising coupons during the first year of sales. (Yes, the result was a loss.) Coca-Cola realized the power of the mass media long before many other, much longer established companies. It has always advertised with gusto.

Shortly before he died in 1888, Pemberton and his son sold the rights to Coca-Cola to Asa Candler (1851–1929). Candler, later mayor of Atlanta, was also an advertising enthusiast (as well as a doctor, pharmacist, property developer, and entrepreneur).

While Coke's advertising attracted customers, the packaging of the product was also used to market it. Progress brought the curvaceous Coke bottle, one of the great images of the twentieth century. Of course,

Coca-Cola's prewar sloganizing has stood the test of time.

1886:	Drink Coca-Cola
1904:	Delicious and Refreshing
1905:	Coca-Cola Revives and Sustains
1906:	The Great National Temperance Drink
1917:	Three Million a Day
1922:	Thirst Knows No Season
1925:	Six Million a Day
1927:	Around the Corner from Everywhere
1929:	The Pause That Refreshes
1932:	Ice-Cold Sunshine
1938:	The Best Friend Thirst Ever Had
1939:	Coca-Cola Goes Along
1942:	Wherever You Are, Whatever You Do, Wherever You May Be, When You Think of Refreshment, Think of Ice-Cold Coca-Cola
1942:	The Only Thing Like Coca-Cola Is Coca-Cola Itself. It's The Real Thing.

Coke hasn't actually used the bottle for a number of years, but it is indelibly imprinted in our minds. Indeed, when you buy a can of Coke, there is still a picture of the bottle, just to remind you of its beauty.

The bottle was the result of a design competition held in 1915 and won by the Root Glass Company. (The competition, of course, was a smart marketing ploy.) The Coke president, Asa Candler, said: "We need a bottle which a person will recognize as Coca-Cola even when he feels it in the dark." The bottle differentiated the brand and added to the brand's identity. (Coca-Cola didn't become available in cans until 1955.)

THE GREATEST LESSONS

Sell, sell, sell.   Soft drink, hard sell has been the central dichotomy of Coca-Cola's existence. Selling is its modus operandi.

Push and promote. According to the records, Coca-Cola's first ad appeared a mere three weeks after Pemberton invented the drink. Presumably the decision-making chain was quite a short one. The ad ran in the *Atlanta Journal* and proclaimed: "Coca-Cola. Delicious! Refreshing! Exhilarating! Invigorating! The New Pop Soda Fountain Drink, containing the properties of the wonderful Coca plant and the famous Cola nuts." Later, Coke advertisements claiming that the drink was "delicious and refreshing" were featured in Georgia school reports. Among Asa Candler's initiatives was the distribution of thousands of vouchers offering free glasses of the drink.

Establish positive associations. Crucial to Coca-Cola's success were the positive associations emphasized by its ads and promotions. Coca-Cola's sales pitch was all-American. Some early ads featured baseball star Ty Cobb and other ads provided idyllic views of American life. In 1931 Coke took this approach further by portraying Father Christmas as an enthusiastic drinker.

Great Decision #14

*During the 1920s, Matsushita was a struggling young business and its latest
product, a bicycle light, was initially unsuccessful. Then Konosuke
Matsushita ordered salespeople to leave a working light in each store they
visited. It was a brilliantly simple marketing decision. Seeing the light at
work changed people's perceptions. Sales took off, and so did the company.*

"We are going to win and the industrial West is going to lose out;
there's not much you can do about it because the reasons for your failure are within yourselves," said Konosuke Matsushita (1894–1989), in
one of the most chilling passages in management literature for Western
managers.[3] Matsushita mapped out why the West was destined to lose
and the Japanese were inevitably going to emerge victorious in the battle
for industrial supremacy, and he did so from a position of immense
strength.

Yet Matsushita's origins were humble. Matsushita grew up in poverty in a small village near Wakayama. He had seven brothers and sisters.
His once relatively prosperous family lived in straitened circumstances
after his father lost money betting on commodities. Matsushita left
school in 1904 and was apprenticed to a maker of charcoal grills. He later
worked his way up to become an inspector in the Osaka Electric Light
Company and, in 1917, founded his own company, Matsushita Electric.

Matsushita's first product was a plug adapter. He had suggested the
idea to his previous employer but they had shown no interest. This was
hardly surprising because Matsushita had little idea of how to actually
make the product. It took Matsushita four months, working with four
colleagues, to figure out how to make the adapters. No one bought them.

Matsushita's first break came as order to made insulator plates. The
order was filled on time and the products were high-quality. Matsushita
began to make money. He then developed an innovative bicycle light.
Again, retailers were unimpressed. Then Matsushita had his salespeople
leave a switched-on light in each shop they called on. This simple product demonstration impressed customers, and the business took off. By
1932 Matsushita had over 1,000 employees, 10 factories, and 280 patents.
Matsushita's decision to show retailers and customers how his product
worked provided the initial basis for his business empire.

During the Second World War, Matsushita made ships and planes as part of the Japanese war effort, even though he had no experience in either area. In 1958 Matsushita Electric was given an award for the quality of its factory operations and, in 1990, Matsushita bought MCA (a year after Sony bought Columbia Pictures). This is a cruelly abbreviated version of how Matsushita created a $42 billion business from nothing. He also created one of the world's most successful brands, Panasonic, and amassed a personal fortune of $3 billion.

THE GREATEST LESSONS

Seeing is believing. If your product is innovative and different, customers need assistance in understanding its possibilities. Show them. Matsushita believed in making products that had clear, practical benefits and uses. "Don't sell customers goods that they are attracted to. Sell them goods that will benefit them," he said. "After-sales service is more important than assistance before sales. It is through such service that one gets permanent customers."[4]

Expect quality and efficiency. Matsushita admired Henry Ford and emphasized efficient production and quality products: "To be out of stock is due to carelessness. If this happens, apologize to the customers, ask for their address and tell them that you will deliver the goods immediately."

Philosophize. Matsushita admired Henry Ford, but also mapped out the broader spiritual aims he believed a business should have. Profit was not enough. "The mission of a manufacturer should be to overcome poverty, to relieve society as a whole from misery, and bring it wealth." Matsushita's "basic management objective," coined in 1929, said: "Recognizing our responsibilities as industrialists, we will devote ourselves to the progress and development of society and the well-being of people through our business activities, thereby enhancing the quality of life throughout the world."

Failure to make a profit was regarded by Matsushita as "a sort of crime against society. We take society's capital, we take their people, we take their materials, yet without a good profit, we are using precious resources that could be better used elsewhere."

Utilize intelligence. To Matsushita, business was demanding, serious, and crucial: "Business, we know, is now so complex and difficult, the survival of firms so hazardous in an environment increasingly unpredictable, competitive and fraught with danger, that their continued existence depends on the day-to-day mobilization of every ounce of intelligence." Matsushita knew all about the value of intellectual capital, long before it became a fashionable management theory.

Great Decision #15

In 1961 the world's best-selling toy got a playmate. It was a brilliantly success-ful brand extension. Ken became Barbie's partner for life and the toymaker, Mattel, has been extending the Barbie brand ever since.

Who would have thought it? In the age of Nintendo, Play Stations, and an endless array of videos, dolls are still childhood fixtures. Children may trot off to zap a few monsters from outer space for a while, but they always come back to their dolls. Dolls—even the word has a faintly dated ring to it—are universal. Boys are instantly transported into the Marines when handed an Action Man or GI Joe; girls run their hands through their hair and proclaim their independence when handed a Barbie. Dolls are big business.

Just look at the marketing jamboree to celebrate the fortieth birth-day of Barbie, often said to be the most successful toy in history. Early in 1999, the world rejoiced. "Forty years of dreams," proclaimed Barbie's makers, Mattel. Dream on. Forty or not, Barbie defies the aging process in a defiantly old-fashioned sort of way. No cellulite in sight, Barbie has long legs and a figure as shapely as shapely could be. Translated from doll size into reality, Barbie would stand seven feet tall with five-foot long legs. Her stats would be 40-22-36. One might have thought that the sex-ist freak show Barbie-style would now be outdated. Not so. A Barbie doll is bought every two seconds. That's one billion and counting. Barbie, who first saw the light of day at the annual Toy Fair in New York in 1959, is now a $1.9 billion industry. Dolly gosh indeed.

Barbie (real name: Barbara Millicent Roberts) was the idea of Ruth Handler, wife of one of the founders of Mattel. Mrs. Handler saw her daughter—named Barbara, as it happens—playing with paper dolls and was inspired to make something a little more permanent and realistic. "If a little girl was going to do role-playing of what she would be like at 16 or 17, it was a little stupid to play with a doll that had a flat chest. So I gave her beautiful breasts," said Mrs. Handler. The breasts haven't always worked in Barbie's favor. In Japan sales were initially sluggish. Market research found that girls and their parents thought that Barbie's breasts were too large. By Japanese standards they were. Mattel eventually changed the doll for the Japanese market. The licensee in Japan quickly sold two million of the smaller-breasted Barbies.

The longevity of dolls is, somewhat strangely perhaps, an object lesson in modern management. Consultant Ian Ritchie of the Oxford Group has worked with toymaker Hasbro and identifies a number of key lessons from the toy business. "Getting toys to market as fast as possible is critical. The time it takes to get from an idea to the shelves of a toy store can be the difference between success and failure," he says. "Then there is the question of timing. In the doll market the timing has to be exactly right—you have to ensure that the dolls which support the fashionable film, book, or TV series are available at exactly the right time." Hasbro has moved to a far greater degree of teamworking in developing its products than many other companies. Teams now involve people from different departments working together to speed up product improvements, design, and delivery. The time it takes to get one of the company's products to market has been reduced by as much as 70 percent.

Then there is the question of line extensions. Doll makers are masters at extending their brands further and further still. While Barbie is a universal and (usually) standardized product, part of its success has been the number of costume variations available. Over 100 new costumes are added each year. This is necessary, because Barbie is a Renaissance woman. You can have it all. "She's a successful businesswoman, a member of a rock band, and a Women's World Cup Soccer Player," Barbie's Web site informs us. She also has a man in her life—Ken. He is suitably coincidental, a real brand extension. Introduced in 1961, Ken has lurked in the background, presumably content to watch Barbie make such a success of her multifaceted life. The decision to extend the Barbie brand through the introduction of Ken laid the foundation for an entire series of extensions that have kept the Barbie brand in the limelight.

Barbie also has a friend, Midge, who first saw the light of day in 1963, slipped into obscurity for years, then made a stunning comeback in 1988. In 1964 came Skipper, Barbie's little-known younger sister. In 1968 Barbie crossed cultural frontiers with her black friend, Christie; then in 1988 a Hispanic friend, Teresa, became Barbie's confidante. These friends were followed by Kira, Barbie's Asian friend in 1992; Barbie's much younger sister, Stacie; the unfeasibly young sister, Kelly; and, in 1997, Becky, who is confined to a wheelchair.

THE GREATEST LESSONS

Brand extensions allow companies to get more mileage out of a basic idea and keep the product fresh.   Jumble sales are full of dolls that failed to move with the times. Hasbro's Action Man first saw the light of day in 1964 and has now been seen in over 350 different manifestations. The 12-inch warrior has been a polar explorer, space ranger, atomic man, life-guard, desert fighter, and football player.

Products must evolve.   Barbie has embraced virtually every sad and temporary fashion with something approaching abandon. Barbie was inspired by the Beatles, then became, of all things, a Mod. Along the way, she has also reflected the "prairie look"—whatever that may be—and gotten into disco music. In the 1980s, she got into power dressing but still found time to be an aerobics instructor. The sporting theme has continued: The late twentieth-century Barbie is a basketball and soccer player.

Mattel pronounces its pride in Barbie's multicareer approach. "Barbie has the unique ability to inspire self-esteem, glamour, and a sense of adventure in all who love her," the company gushes. "She has been a role model to women as an astronaut in 1994, 1986, and in 1965—nearly 20 years before Sally Ride! As a college graduate in 1963, surgeon in 1973, business executive in 1986, Summit Diplomat and airline pilot in 1990, a presidential candidate in 1992, and a dentist in 1997, the Barbie doll has opened new dreams for girls that were not as accessible in the early 1960s. As a matter of fact, the world's most popular fashion doll has actually had 75 careers since her inception." Unfortunately, Mattel does not record the success of the Summit Diplomat version.

Evolution means that Barbie now comes complete with 15,000 combinations. Change the outfit, the eyes, the color—but don't even think about changing the legs.

Great Decision #16

Segmentation is one of the cornerstones of marketing. Its modern roots can be traced back to Alfred P. Sloan's decision at General Motors to provide a model of car aimed at each segment of the market.

In 1908, William Crapo Durant (1861–1947) founded the General Motors Company of New Jersey. Less than half a century later, in the early 1950s, the company's Charles E. Wilson told the U.S. Senate Armed Forces Committee: "What is good for the country is good for General Motors and what's good for General Motors is good for the country." At the time, there were few dissenters to such sentiments. For much of the twentieth century, GM stood as a symbol of the might of corporate America.

GM's stature can, to a significant degree, be attributed to Alfred P. Sloan (1875–1966), who was the company's legendary chief during its formative years. Researching her case study of GM for *The Change Masters,* Rosabeth Moss Kanter was told by then GM chairman Roger Smith that his aim was to "return this company to the way Sloan intended it to be managed"—and that was more than 30 years after Sloan's death.[5]

Sloan was general manager of the Hyatt Roller Bearing Company at the age of 24 and became president when it merged with United Motors, which in turn became part of General Motors in 1917. Initially a director and vice-president, Sloan became GM's chief executive in 1946 and was honorary chairman from 1956 until his death.

When Sloan took over General Motors, the fledgling automobile market was dominated by Ford. Ford had become a pioneer of mass production techniques. In 1920 Ford was making a car a minute and the famously black Model T accounted for 60 percent of the market. General Motors managed to scrimp and scrap its way to around 12 percent.

With Ford cornering the mass market, the accepted wisdom was that the only alternative for competitors lay in the negligibly-sized luxury market. Sloan thought otherwise and concentrated GM's attentions on the as yet nonexistent, middle market. His aim was a car for "every purse and every purpose."

At the time, GM was an unwieldy combination of companies with eight models that basically competed against each other as well as against

Ford. Sloan cut the eight models down to five and decided that rather than competing with each other, each model would be targeted at a particular segment of the market. "Back then, if you said the word *Pontiac,* any consumer in the country could tell you what kind of person drove it," said *BusinessWeek.* The five GM models—Chevrolet, Oldsmobile, Pontiac, Buick, and Cadillac—were to be updated and changed regularly and came in more than one color. Ford continued to offer functional, reliable cars; GM offered choice.

"GM's divisions kept customers buying GM cars every year throughout their entire lives, offering variety where Ford produced a car of any color the consumer wanted, as long as it was black," says author Peter Cohan.[6]

THE GREATEST LESSONS

Understand your market.   Sloan understood the aspirations and expectations of his market in the way that Henry Ford did when he started out in business.

Change constantly.   Yesterday's model is history. Sloan proved that the public has an appetite for constant change and for following fashions. Newness is good for business.

Great Decision #17

The Grateful Dead established immense customer loyalty during the 1980s when they decided to allow fans to tape their concerts. The result? In 1996 sales of merchandise were around $50 million, and 100,000 people visit the group's Internet site every day.

Everyone in business has been told that success is all about attracting and retaining customers. Such words of wisdom are soon forgotten. Once companies have attracted customers, they often overlook the second half of the equation. They forget what they regard as the humdrum side of business—ensuring that the customer remains a customer.

Failing to concentrate on retaining, as well as attracting, customers costs businesses huge amounts of money annually. It has been estimated that the average company loses between 10 and 30 percent of its customers every year. In our constantly changing markets, this is not surprising. What is surprising is the fact that few companies have any idea how many customers they have lost.

Only now are organizations beginning to wake up to these lost opportunities and calculate the financial implications. Reducing the number of customers a company loses can make a radical difference in its performance. Research in the United States showed that a 5 percent decrease in the number of defecting customers led to profit increases of between 25 and 85 percent.

Xerox takes the question of retaining customers so seriously that customer retention is a key part of the company's bonus scheme. In the United States, Domino's Pizza estimates that a regular customer is worth more than $5,000 over ten years. A customer who receives a poor-quality product or service on the first visit and as a result never returns, costs the company thousands of dollars in potential revenue (more if you consider how many people they are liable to tell about their bad experience).

If you want lessons in loyalty, it is worth looking at some unlikely sources. Try Jerry Garcia, Chief Marketing Officer. The Grateful Dead frontman created a successful business empire. Not bad for a devout hippie and drug user. In 1994 the band had revenues of around $95 million, selling about $50 million worth of tickets, making around $35 million from merchandising, and selling a few CDs along the way. You begin to see why those other hippie capitalists, Ben and Jerry, named an ice cream flavor after Garcia.

Why is the Grateful Dead a source of broader inspiration? For a number of reasons.

First, the group established tremendous customer loyalty. Fans were allowed to tape their concerts and were given easier access to tickets through a mail-order service. The group's employees were also loyal. The same crew stayed with them as they traveled around. Even when the band wasn't touring, the crew were paid, and paid well. There was virtually no staff turnover or absenteeism. The message for other companies is that if you look after your people, they will look after your customers in the same way.

The next thing the Grateful Dead did was to extend its brand. People who sold products outside the concerts were brought in as official licensees. They became part of the team, and both sides got rich. Now you can buy Grateful Dead golf balls and baby clothes.

Finally, the band gave people access to the brand. They preferred touring rather than producing lots of records. They insisted on quality rather than quantity. People identified with them.[7]

The Grateful Dead topped all this with a very strong image. Their product was different and they played by different rules. This meant that they didn't slavishly follow fashion. They didn't appear to be in business to rip people off or even to make money, and yet make money they did.

The Grateful Dead's singer Jerry Garcia died, but still the brand plays on—and there are a lot of people still playing tapes of Dead concerts.

THE GREATEST LESSONS

Give respect where it's due.   The Grateful Dead gave their fans respect. They decided that it wasn't in their interest to rip off their fans and it wasn't in the interest of the fans to rip off the band. Grown-up marketing.

Loyalty is cheap; the dividends are enormous.   Engendering loyalty among Deadheads didn't cost the band a great deal—the only cost was potential short-term revenue losses. But it bore fruit in the long term.

Relationships count.   The route to customer retention is relationship marketing: nurturing relationships with customers that create loyalty.

Relationship-building programs now cover a multitude of activities, from customer magazines to vouchers and gifts. Basically, they aim to persuade a person to use a preferred vendor in order to take advantage of the benefits offered, whether the benefit is a trip to Acapulco or a price-reduction voucher for a calorie-controlled canned drink. Skeptics may mutter that there is nothing new in this. Indeed, businesses have been giving long-standing customers discounts and inducements since time immemorial. What is different now is the highly organized way in which companies are attempting to build relationships and customer loyalty.

Great Decision #18

In the 1950s, Philip Morris decided to reposition Marlboro as a man's ciga-
rette. The Marlboro cowboy helped create one of the world's most successful
and durable brands.

In the 1950s, the tobacco company R.J. Reynolds had reason to feel
complacent. Its market share was approaching 35 percent. It was the
dominant force in the American cigarette industry. Among those trailing
breathlessly behind—in sixth place—was Philip Morris, whose market
share was less than 10 percent. Executives at R.J. Reynolds no doubt laid
back in their executive-style chairs and inhaled deeply on one of their
successful products.

Meanwhile, plans were being hatched at Philip Morris. They
smacked of desperation. One of its brands, Marlboro, was targeted at
female smokers. It had first been launched in the 1920s with the suitably
feminine slogan, "Mild as May." During the Second World War, Marlboro
production halted as Camel, Lucky Strike, and Chesterfield dominated
the market. In the heavy-smoking fifties, those three brands dominated.

Marlboro was brought back on the market in the early 1950s but
remained a woman's cigarette. Fear of lung cancer was growing and
Marlboro was filtered. Men regarded Marlboro's filters as effeminate.

Philip Morris brought in the Leo Burnett ad agency to determine
how it could make Marlboro appealing to men as well as women. The
result was a 1955 ad campaign based around a tattooed man. The
Marlboro smoker was reincarnated "as a lean, relaxed outdoorsman—a
cattle rancher, a Navy officer, a flyer—whose tattooed wrist suggested a
romantic past, a man who had once worked with his hands, who knew
the score, who merited respect." Marlboro sales exploded. In New York,
sales increased 5,000 percent in eight months.

The original Marlboro man was very talkative—he had quite a lot of
explaining to do. He cheerfully gave his life story in the early ads ("I'm a
rancher. Grew up in this part of the country ...") but lapsed into silence
in later years. The brand's development was helped by a strongly
designed box with recognizable colors. The box was the membership
card. You, too, became a cowboy if you carried one—even if you lived in
the middle of the city and wouldn't know one end of a cow from the
other.

By 1989, Marlboro accounted for a quarter of all American cigarette sales; Philip Morris had 43 percent of the U.S. market. All was well in Marlboro country, but only for a while, as the drama of what became known as Marlboro Friday lurked around the corner.

THE GREATEST LESSONS

There is always a chance. At the beginning of the 1950s, Marlboro was nowhere, seemingly destined for life as a peripheral brand. Clever and repeated advertising changed its role in life virtually overnight.

Branding is incredibly powerful. Marlboro is more than a brand. It is an international product, name, and image known the world over. Its distinctive red and white colors and its advertising featuring romantic images of the classic American cowboy are recognized universally.

MARLBORO FRIDAY

On April 2, 1993, the U.S. tobacco giant Philip Morris cut the price of its branded cigarettes, including Marlboro, by 25 percent. A day earlier, people might have thought the company was joking, but this was deadly serious. Just over a year later, on June 19, 1994, Michael Miles, the man who made the decision, resigned as chairman and chief executive of Philip Morris. The story behind what has become known as Marlboro Friday raises many of the vital questions that lie at the heart of branding and brand management in modern business.

Marlboro and others in the Philip Morris product line had suffered from long-term loss of market share to generic (unbranded) cigarettes. (It is worth remembering that Philip Morris also produces the cheaper cigarettes that were undermining Marlboro, but that the profit margins on those brands are understandably smaller.) Before Marlboro Friday, the unbranded cigarettes had claimed almost 40 percent of the U.S. market. Selling at half the price of Marlboro, the cheaper competitors, along with RJR Nabisco's Camel brand, had sliced Marlboro's U.S. market share from nearly 30 percent to just over 22 percent. Michael Miles decided that something needed to be done.

Miles had been described as "aloof and uncommunicative." *Fortune* had labeled him "a business junkie … pragmatic, ruthless, focused … cold blooded." He was also a nonsmoker and his experience was in the food side of Philip Morris's massive business empire, in which 1993 sales totaled $61 billion. His food-based background, legend would have it, meant that Miles lacked real enthusiasm for the brand and didn't understand the tobacco business and what Marlboro stood for. With market share falling, the normal solution would have been an advertising blitz or a small price cut, or perhaps both. They might have prodded Marlboro's market share in the right direction.

Miles's solution was more dramatic and unexpected: a massive price cut. Cutting the price of the world's leading cigarette by a fourth to increase flagging market share was a very high-risk gamble indeed. To many commentators, observers, and analysts, it was a strategy driven by panic rather than by long-term considerations.

In addition to making cigarettes cheaper, Marlboro Friday had other, wider-ranging consequences. In one fell swoop it brought to an end the romantic veneration of brands that had evolved during the 1980s. Instead of being seen as secure money-making machines, brands were suddenly unclothed as fallible, potential victims, no matter what their size. There was an outbreak of realism. During the 1980s brands had grown largely, in many cases, due to premium pricing, fueled by annual price increases, often up to 15 percent. The succession of price increases had, in many markets, driven customers into the hands of competitors; hence the growth in own-label goods.

Marlboro Friday marked a new and none-too-welcoming dawn. The stock markets responded with disbelief, as they often do when caught totally unprepared. Philip Morris' shares plummeted 23 percent in one day. (In a final insult to Michael Miles, they rose immediately after his departure.)

Miles's strategy was basically straightforward. He recognized that the company could not continue to charge a premium price for the Marlboro brand, a price that was clearly regarded by many consumers as excessive. Perhaps with an eye to what Compaq had done in PCs, Miles sought to reduce prices and utilize the immense strength of the brand to drive up market share.

In fact, Miles's strategy worked. In the initial period after Marlboro Friday, Philip Morris shares largely recovered and the company grew its total share of the U.S. tobacco market from 42 percent to 46 percent, with Marlboro alone growing from 22 percent to 27 percent. In July 1994, Philip Morris was able to report a 17.6 percent surge in after-tax profits, to $1.23 billion in its second quarter alone. More significant was the fact that this was the first increase in profits recorded since Marlboro Friday. Sales were up by nearly 22 percent in the United States, giving Morris 46.6 percent market share (up 5 percent) while Marlboro reached a record 28.5 percent (up 6.5 percent).

What eventually finished Miles's career with Philip Morris was his plan to separate the company's two core businesses—tobacco and food and drinks (including Maxwell House, Kraft, and Miller beer). This met with opposition from former chairman Hamish Maxwell, who had masterminded the company's diversification in the 1980s through strategic buys such as General Foods, Kraft, and Jacobs Suchard.

Again, Miles's logic was clear. Maxwell had built up the food side of the company's business in the 1980s when it seemed that tobacco was likely to be a declining and potentially troublesome business to be in. The strategy worked to the extent that the food side of Philip Morris accounted for almost half of its turnover by 1993, though it was far from being as profitable as tobacco. Miles had actually become part of Morris when it took over Kraft, where he has been chairman and chief executive. Experienced in the foods business, he was keen to divide the two empires. He was also reacting to the intense antismoking lobby in the United States and to the threat of litigation.

After a six-hour board meeting, Miles's plan was rejected. His position made untenable, he left only weeks later, to be replaced by two smokers from the tobacco side of Philip Morris's business. In Marlboro country, the smokers still ruled the corporate roost.

Great Decision #19

In 1892 Henry Heinz of the H.J. Heinz food company decided the company needed a slogan. He came up with "57 varieties" to describe the foods sold by the company. This was one of the few cases of successful underselling—Heinz produced 60 products at the time—but one that has stood the test of time.

Henry John Heinz (1844–1916) was born in Pittsburgh. He was a precocious entrepreneur: At the age of eight (or twelve, depending on which history book you read) he was selling surplus homegrown vegetables. This enterprise quickly mushroomed (as it were) into an empire. By 1860, Heinz was delivering three wagons full of vegetables to Pittsburgh grocers every week.

Heinz's business continued to grow, and in 1869 he went into a partnership selling, of all things, grated horseradish. The horseradish was notable for its purity; Henry wasn't tempted to add turnip, as others did. This was demonstrated by packaging the product in a clear jar. The partnership went bankrupt six years later, the failure caused by a surfeit of crops that lowered prices. Undaunted, Heinz bounced back and launched F. & J. Heinz, with his brother and cousin as partners and himself as the manager, in 1876. The new company made pickles and condiments. One of its first products was tomato ketchup.

In 1888 the company was reestablished as H.J. Heinz and in 1892, Henry Heinz decided the company needed a slogan. He came up with "57 varieties" to describe the foods sold by the company. This was one of the few cases of modest marketing—Heinz produced 60 products at the time—but one that has stood the test of time. Heinz was a born marketer. "It's not so much what you say but how, when, and where," he sagely observed.

The company was incorporated in 1905 with Henry as president. Heinz's business philosophy was straight out of a Victorian philanthropist's guidebook: "Heart power is better than horse power," he said. His factory by the Allegheny River was something of a model for the way in which people were treated and for its cleanliness. Heinz initiated factory tours to show off the factory to interested parties. At the time of his death in 1916, the company employed thousands of people at 25 factories.

It was not until 1965, when R. Burt Gookin became CEO, that the Heinz family relinquished control of the top job. Gookin was followed by former Irish rugby international Tony O'Reilly. Some things didn't change. "My acid test ... is whether a housewife, intending to buy Heinz tomato ketchup in a store, finding it to be out of stock, will walk out of the store to buy it elsewhere or switch to an alternative product," said Tony O'Reilly.[8]

Along the way, Heinz acquired StarKist (1963), Ore-Ida (1965), and Weight Watchers International (1978). Heinz is now on only its sixth CEO; William R. Johnson took on the top job in 1998. The contemporary Heinz company has a market capitalization of $18.5 billion, over 40,000 employees, and markets more than 5,000 varieties in over 200 countries.

THE GREATEST LESSONS

Think international.   Henry Heinz had bold ambitions. "Our market is the world," he proclaimed with customary gusto. In search of new markets, he visited Europe. Famously, he turned up at London's prestigious Fortnum & Mason store with five cases of goods. After tasting the samples, the Fortnum & Mason purchaser is reputed to have said: "I think, Mr. Heinz, we will take the lot." By 1900, Heinz salespeople were selling the company's range of 200 products throughout the world. It was claimed that they visited "every inhabited continent."

Continue the legacy.   Heinz has proved adept at handing the baton from one generation to the next. Current CEO William Johnson echoes the founder's commitment. Johnson champions an equation for success called V5V: "Heinz will achieve success through the five Vs: a vision based on global category management and growth; a voracious appetite for success; an unyielding focus on enhancing shareholder value; a dedication to volume growth fueled by cost containment; and a high-velocity commitment to change."

Pay your debts.   Heinz paid off all his creditors when he was bankrupted. This took time, but it engendered the goodwill that helped his next venture prosper.

Great Decision #20

William Hoover placed an ad in the local newspaper offering a free ten-day trial use to anyone who submitted a written request for his new sweeper. Rather than sending the sweeper direct, Hoover sent the sweeper to a reputable store near the requester's home. Hoover included a note, asking the store to deliver it and, if a sale was made, telling the store to keep the commission. This not only secured direct sales, it helped Hoover quickly establish a large network of dealers. A brand was born.

William H. Hoover was born in 1849 in Lancaster County, Pennsylvania. In 1875, Hoover purchased the John Lind tannery in what is now North Canton, Ohio. There he relocated his family and his business, which was eventually renamed the W. H. Hoover Company.

Hoover's wife's cousin, Murray Spangler, was the night janitor at a Canton department store. An asthma sufferer, Spangler set out to find a way to keep dust from rising while he was sweeping floors. With a tin box, a fan, a pillow case, and a broom handle, he fashioned a crude, 40-pound device that pulled the dust away from him while he swept. The vacuum cleaner was born.

Spangler approached the Hoovers for financial backing to build and market the device. With a product endorsement from his wife, who had tried the device in the family home, William Hoover purchased the patent from Spangler in 1908 and incorporated the Hoover Suction Sweeper Company. Spangler was retained as plant supervisor to help establish manufacturing operations and, in the first year, six employees built and sold nearly 350 "suction sweepers."

Electric cleaners were at first a sideline for the W.H. Hoover Company. A room in the leather goods factory was used for their manufacture, and the entire workforce numbered fewer than 20 people. The plant's capacity was six to eight cleaners a day.

In 1907, Hoover made a decision that would make the Hoover brand synonymous with the words *vacuum cleaner*. He placed an ad in the local newspaper offering a free ten-day trial use to anyone who submitted a written request. Rather than sending the sweeper directly to those who answered the ad, Hoover sent the sweeper to a reputable store near the requester's home. He included a note, asking the store to deliver the sweeper to the person and, if a sale was made, telling the store to keep the commission. This not only secured direct sales, it helped Hoover quickly establish a large network of dealers.

In 1909, the development of the small high-speed fractional horse-power universal motor by Hamilton and Beach of Racine, Wisconsin helped reduce the weight of the sweeper. Then Hoover established an engineering and design program of its own. Among its results was the development of the principle of carpet vibration for removal of dust. The original work on this principle was later developed to give Hoover cleaners an exclusive feature—the gentle beating or tapping of the carpet by a spiral agitator bar to loosen embedded dirt and grit. Added to the brushing action by revolving brushes and strong suction, this produced Hoover's famous "triple action," and inspired the well-known slogan: "It beats, as it sweeps, as it cleans."

Hoover's fame soon spread beyond America. In 1911, he opened a Canadian assembly plant. Eight years later, he began a sales organization in England. Meanwhile, the automobile was replacing the horse and buggy and the demand for harnesses and leather goods steadily declined. By 1919, it was decided to discontinue that part of the business, and the Hoover Suction Sweeper Company (later shortened to the Hoover Company) centered all its attention on the manufacture and sale of vacuum sweepers.

Hoover died on February 25, 1932. Hoover continues to be one of the most recognized brand names in the world.

THE GREATEST LESSONS

Think ahead. Not many businesspeople can smell change in the air and then do something about it. Most sniff contentedly and carry on as before, or bury their heads in the sand. Few companies are willing to admit that there is no future in their business. William Hoover was one of the most notable exceptions. His farsighted recognition that cars would soon kill his business that made leather accessories for horse-drawn carriages led to the 1908 creation of the Electric Suction Sweeper Company. Hoover's new enterprise created the mass market vacuum cleaner and provided a (largely ignored) blueprint for moving with the times.

Get retailers on your side.   Hoover could have bypassed retailers and so avoided paying them a commission. In the interests of long-term development, however, he brought them into the process. They became his allies.

Great Decision #21

In 1981, a group of 13 senior Harley-Davidson executives led by Vaughn Beals bought the company. They celebrated with a victory ride from the company's factory in York, Pennsylvania to its headquarters in Milwaukee. Then they made a great decision: The new owners started the Harley Owners Group (H.O.G.) to get customers more involved with the brand. It worked.

Freedom and individualism stand at the heart of the Harley-Davidson brand. The Milwaukee-based motorcycle company's greatest assets are a romanticized version of its past and the intensely loyal customers who perpetuate this romanticism. For Harley, the past began in Milwaukee at the turn of the twentieth century, when a young man named William Harley, 21, and his friend Arthur Davidson, 20, began experiments on "taking the work out of bicycling." They were joined by Arthur's brothers, Walter and William.

Many changes were made to the engine design before its builders were satisfied. (The familiar 45-degree V-twin wasn't introduced until 1909.) With the design of the looped frame, they began production in 1903. Harley-Davidson erected its first building at the current Juneau Avenue site in 1906 and was incorporated in 1907. The total output that year was 150 motorcycles. By the time the famous V-twin went into production two years later, the company was cranking out more than 1,100 motorcycles a year.

Harley models dominated racing events in the United States, and its motorcycles were used by the American military, having proven their worth in border skirmishes with Pancho Villa. By the 1920s, Harley-Davidson was the largest motorcycle manufacturer in the world and was exporting to dealers in 67 countries.

The roaring 1920s brought many of the innovations that became Harley trademarks, including the tear drop petrol tank and the novel addition of a front brake. The Wall Street crash of 1929 took its toll on motorcycle sales, but the company bounced back with the introduction of its EL model, known as the Knucklehead. The Sportster (1957), the Duo Glide (1958), and the Electra Glide (1965) followed.

After struggling against Japanese competition during the 1960s and 1970s, the company turned a corner in the 1980s. In 1981, a group of 13 senior Harley executives led by Vaughn Beals bought the company. They celebrated with a victory ride from the company's factory in York, Pennsylvania to its headquarters in Milwaukee. The new owners started the Harley Owners Group (H.O.G.) to get customers more involved with the brand. In 1993, the company celebrated its 90th anniversary with more than 100,000 Harley enthusiasts converging on Milwaukee for a drive-through parade featuring 60,000 Harley-Davidson machines.

THE GREATEST LESSONS

Love the product.   How many management teams really use and love their products? Not many. The management team's victory ride was a ringing endorsement of Harley's product, a powerful statement of commitment.

Connect with customers.   The Harley Owners Group has 325,000 members. This number is likely to grow: Harley hopes to increase production from 118,000 in 1996 to between 200,000 and 300,000 by the company's centenary in 2003.

Move on.   Harley uses the past rather than being stuck in the past. When CEO Richard Teerlink climbed into the saddle at Harley-Davidson in 1989, he inherited one of the strongest brand images in the world. Brand loyalty among dedicated Harley enthusiasts remained unshakable, but the company was on the slide. Quality had become an issue as the famous brand tried to get costs down to compete with aggressive Japanese competitors. To add insult to injury, the Japanese were stealing a slice of the market for custom cruising bikes with machines modeled on the Harley blueprint.

Teerlink keyed into Harley's greatest asset—the people who care about the Harley-Davidson brand. He opened a dialogue outside the company with its loyal customer base and inside the company with its workforce.

Make quality an issue.   Teerlink also introduced a rigorous new quality regime to ensure that what left the factory was worthy of the Harley-Davidson name. This meant that customers sometimes had to wait to take delivery of their new motorcycles, but it guaranteed that the machine they received would be worth the wait.

Attract new customers. Don't get stuck in the past.   Today, the average age of a Harley customer is 42, compared to 32 ten years ago. The brand is benefiting from a new breed of professional—accountants and lawyers who don motorcycle leathers on the weekend in search of freedom and a life away from the office. (The number of customers buying their first motorcycle or coming back to riding after a lapse increased more than threefold between 1987 and 1994). Orders outstrip production, creating a waiting list for many models. One-year-old Harleys sell for 25 percent more than the list price of brand new ones.

In 1995, Harley introduced the Heritage Springer Softail, laying claim to the future with its own special branding of the past. In 1997, the company enjoyed record sales of $1.75 billion, on 132,000 motorcycles, and commanded a hefty 48 percent share of the North American market for heavy road bikes.

Great Decision #22

During the Second World War, Robert Woodruff, president of Coca-Cola, committed to selling bottles of Coke to members of the armed services for a nickel a bottle. Customer loyalty never came cheaper.

The Second World War was one of the great watershed events in history and, in particular, in corporate history. Several companies paved the way for their future success through wholehearted commitment to the cause.

Consider Nestlé and Nescafé. The development of Nescafé, the first water-soluble coffee, took research scientists at Nestlé's laboratories in Vevey, Switzerland eight long years. In 1930 the Brazilian Coffee Institute got in touch with then Nestlé chief, Louis Dapples. Brazil had a sizable coffee surplus and was anxious to explore ways to sell coffee more successfully. (Great decision: Explore every avenue.) Nestlé got to work out the Brazilian problem, but it was not until 1937 that its scientists were able to bellow the Swiss equivalent of "Eureka!" as they came up with their version of powdered coffee.

The new product was rushed to market quickly after its discovery. During World War II, the entire output of the company's U.S. plant—in excess of one million cases—was reserved for military use. Wartime demand for Nescafé went through the roof, and Nestlé's total sales increased from $100 million to $225 million. Now it is calculated that, every second of every day, 3,000 cups of the world's leading coffee brand are consumed.

Nescafé wasn't the only product to make an impact during wartime. When Allied troops landed in Normandy in 1944 they carried self-heating cans of Heinz soup. Heinz's wartime slogans included the memorable "Beans to bombers" and "Pickles to pursuit planes."

The most notable success, however, was achieved by Coca-Cola. Asa Candler's children eventually sold the Coca-Cola company to another Atlanta businessman, Ernest Woodruff, for the then massive sum of $25 million. In 1923, Ernest's son, Robert Woodruff (1890–1985) became company president. During Woodruff's long tenure—surely one of the longest in corporate history—Coke continued to develop people's awareness of the product. Its Coke Bathing Girls calendars were a fixture in American drug stores during the 1930s. Later Coke looked to the skies:

Returning Apollo astronauts were welcomed with a sign reading, "Welcome back to earth, home of Coca-Cola."

Back on planet earth, a foreign sales department for Coke was set up in 1926. Internationally, its reputation was cemented during the Second World War when it boldly and ambitiously promised that any U.S. soldier would be able to buy a Coke for a nickel. Coke became the symbol of American taste and consumption. To fulfill its promise, Coke built 60 mobile bottling plants and sent them along with the Army. Each could be run by two people and produce 1,370 bottles an hour. (The more cynical slant on this story is that Coke convinced the government that its drink was vital to the well-being and happiness of U.S. troops, to insulate itself from the potential threat of sugar rationing.)

In the postwar years Coke expanded its corporate empire in the quest for what it engagingly called "share of throat." New drinks were added to its range. These included Fanta, Sprite, and TAB. None hit the heights of the original brand.

In the 1970s doubt entered the Coca-Cola empire for the first time. Pepsi-Cola upped the pressure with the Pepsi Challenge. Coke had to open its eyes to the possibility that it had real competition. After a remarkable reign, Woodruff gave way to Roberto Goizueta (1931–1997) in 1981.

Today, more than 900 million Coca-Colas are sold every single day. Coca-Cola is the best-known global soda brand. Currently it is available in virtually every country in the world; the only exceptions are Libya, Iran, and Cuba, where its absence is a matter of politics rather than taste.

THE GREATEST LESSONS

Short-term loss can create long-term loyalty.   The war cemented Coke's place in the hearts of Americans. *Time* magazine celebrated Coke's "peaceful near-conquest of the world." Coke's competitors complained of favoritism and hyperbole. Loyalty can never be won through short-termism. Consider an older decision: Eighteenth-century British banker Thomas Coutts wrote off the royal family's gambling debts to keep them as customers. That was a great loss-leading strategy; Coutts thrives as "the top people's bank" to this day. Her Majesty the Queen is a customer.

Think big.   Humility has never been on the Coca-Cola agenda. One of its publicity handouts noted: "A billion hours ago, human life appeared on Earth. A billion minutes ago, Christianity emerged. A billion seconds ago, the Beatles performed on the *Ed Sullivan Show.* A billion Coca-Colas ago was yesterday morning." No postmodernist irony there.

Great Decision #23

Struggling with your marketing? Create a ranking. Henry Luce's creation of Fortune in 1929 spawned the Fortune 500, which served as the corporate benchmark for the twentieth century—as well as being a clever marketing gimmick for the magazine.

For journalists and readers, rankings are irresistible. Henry Luce (1898–1967) knew a thing or two about them.

Luce was the man behind *Time,* which he founded in 1923, and *Fortune* (1929). The Fortune 500 served as the corporate benchmark of the twentieth century and remains a powerful barometer of who's up and down in the corporate world. Peter Drucker recently claimed that "The Fortune 500 is over," but announcements of its demise appear to be premature.

The Fortune 500 ranking is a brilliant marketing tool. Every single time it is mentioned, we mention the name of Luce's magazine. It associates the magazine with authority, gravitas, and success. At *Time,* Luce provided another approach with the annual person of the year cover story. In effect, this is another ranking.

That such rankings have a hugely powerful influence is evidenced by the success of *BusinessWeek's* biannual ranking of business schools. The issue routinely outsells all other issues of the magazine in the year, as anxious students, deans, and faculty members scour the magazine for their institution's ranking.

Of course, rankings are largely a crass and superficial gimmick. Being the top company in the Fortune 500 is no guarantee of future success, and its measure of current achievement can also be limited—as well as confusing to the casual observer. But as a marketing decision, Luce's idea was imaginative, influential, and long-lasting. I rest my case.

THE GREATEST LESSONS

Give people something that is useful and informative.   The great thing about the Fortune 500 is that people utilize it. What's more, the very people who use it are the people *Fortune* wants to persuade to buy the magazine.

Notes

[1] Kotler, Philip, *Marketing Management,* Prentice Hall, 1994.

[2] Drucker, Peter, *The Practice of Management,* Harper & Row, 1954.

[3] Kotter, John, *Matsushita Leadership,* Free Press, 1997.

[4] Kotter.

[5] Kanter, Rosabeth Moss, *The Change Masters,* Simon & Schuster, 1983.

[6] Cohan, Peter, *Technology Leaders,* Jossey-Bass, 1997.

[7] Hill, Sam, and Rifkin, Glen, *Radical Marketing,* Harper Business, 1999.

[8] Kotler, Philip, *Marketing Management,* Prentice Hall, 1996.

LUCKY FORESIGHT

"At any given moment one is conscious of only a small section of what one knows. Intuition allows one to draw on that vast storehouse of unconscious knowledge that includes not only everything that one has experienced or learned either consciously or subliminally, but also the infinite reservoir of the collection or universal consciousness, in which individual separateness and ego boundaries are transcended," says the psychologist Francis E. Vaughan. Intuition, if Vaughan is to be believed, gives you access to the collective wisdom of civilization, something no software package has so far achieved.

Many great decisions are the result of what might be called lucky foresight. People get it right for inexplicable reasons. They don't run figures through endless databases. They don't analyze, then analyze some more. They just feel that it's right, then they do it. They go with their gut feelings.

That kind of intuition is all-embracing and, as a result, steeped in vagueness. It is inexplicable, but it can explain all. It is a human constant, but capable of disappearing into the ether.

Some of the business world's greatest names quickly reveal steadfast usage of intuition. "You don't have to discuss things. You can sense it. The tingle is as important as the intellect," argued Sir David Simon, then chairman of British Petroleum. On his decision not to elevate Jeffrey Katzenberg to president, Disney chief Michael Eisner said it came down to "a lot of very logical reasons and also some intuitional reasons." "Once I have a feeling for the choices, I have no problems with the decisions," says IBM chief Lou Gerstner. Consider this description of Eisner by Barry Diller, formerly Eisner's boss at ABC and Paramount: "Michael looks like Goofy, and he often acts like Goofy, and he's definitely in the body of Goofy! But he's got one of the most smartly spirited minds that I've ever come across. You can see the electrical charges moving from one

73

point to another in his brain. Spectacular instincts. Of course, he's not always right, and when it comes to that he has a somewhat tractionless memory."[1] "Spectacular instincts" can be worth hundreds of millions of dollars.

Virgin boss Richard Branson is another corporate leader who seems willing and able to follow his instinct for an opportunity. Branson recalls his decision to go into the airline business in 1984: "It was a move which in pure economic terms everybody thought was mad, including my closest friends but it was something which I felt we could bring something to that others were not bringing."[2] It didn't add up, but Branson thought there was something there and persisted. Great decision.

Intuition gives you the confidence to do things you might ordinarily shy away from. Bravado abounds. When Arthur Guinness set up his brewing company in 1759 in an abandoned brewery in Dublin, he knew that he'd succeed. He was so sure that, the story goes, he signed a 9,000-year lease for the premises at £45 per year.

General Electric's Jack Welch is another who has pronounced himself intuitive—or, at least, in touch with his senses. "Here at head office, we don't go very deep into much of anything, but we have a smell of everything," says Welch. "Our job is capital allocation—intellectual and financial. Smell, feel, touch, listen, then allocate. Make bets, with people and dollars. And make mistakes."[3] Go with your gut.

UNDERSTANDING THE GUT

When managers are quizzed about what intuition actually is, they offer a wide range of answers. Researching intuition, Jagdish Parikh of IMD in Switzerland reported that when 1,312 top and senior managers from nine countries were asked, "What is intuition?" they replied in a variety of ways. (What is equally interesting is that each of the responses is credible and plausible. If a manager wishes to view intuition as instinct, you can't really argue the point.)

Research carried out by British academic Phil Hodgson for the book, *What Do High Performance Managers Really Do?* suggests that managers who use their intuition effectively and continuously are likely to have a number of clear characteristics:[4]

- They make decisions quickly and confidently. They are willing to back their judgement and don't spend large periods of time weighing things up.
- They use data only when necessary. Not for them the computer printout containing every single statistic available.
- They recognize intuition as a skill, part of their managerial armory.
- They accept and encourage ideas, whatever their source or apparent usefulness, at every stage.
- They act on intuitive judgements, rather than questioning them.
- They accept no rigid or wrong method of doing things. If something feels, looks, or seems right, they will do it.

WHAT IS INTUITION?[5]

Description	%
Decision/perception without recourse to logical/rational methods	23.4
Inherent perception; inexplicable comprehension; a feeling that comes from within	17.1
Integration of previous experience; processing of accumulated information	16.8
Gut feeling	12.0
Decision/solution to problem, without complete data/facts	8.6
Sixth sense	7.4
Spontaneous perception/vision	7.3
Insight	6.7
Subconscious process	6.1
Instinct	5.7

Great Decision #24

Sony chief Akito Morita noticed that young people liked listening to music wherever they went. He put two and two together and the company developed what became the Walkman, first made in 1980. There was no need for market research. "The public does not know what is possible, we do," said Morita.

Akito Morita (born 1921) was an officer in the Japanese Navy during the Second World War. Trained as a physicist and scientist, Morita could have followed family tradition and gone into sake production. (He refers to himself as "the first son and fifteenth generation heir to one of Japan's finest and oldest sake-brewing families.") Instead, he founded a company with Masaru Ibuka (1908–1997) immediately after the end of the war.

The duo invested the equivalent of £845 and set themselves up in business in a bombed-out Tokyo department store. Here luck and foresight immediately kicked in. When Ibuka and Morita established the Tokyo Tsushin Kogyo company, the first thing they did was write down the company's philosophy. (This in itself is rated as a brave and great decision by Jim Collins, coauthor of *Built to Last*.) The company's initial products did not stand the test of time; Sony's philosophy did. The company stood for something from the very beginning.

Ibuka was the technical expert, Morita the salesman. Tokyo Tsushin Kogyo KK (Tokyo Telecommunications Engineering Corporation) got off to a problematic start. Initially, the company made radio parts and a rice cooker, among other things. Today, Ibuka and Morita's organization is a $45 billion company with over 100,000 employees. According to one Harris poll, Sony is America's most respected brand.

Sony's success is based fundamentally on innovation, an instinctive ability to sniff out market opportunities, and the confidence to pursue them.

In 1949 the company developed magnetic recording tape and in 1950, it sold the first tape recorder in Japan. In 1957 the company produced a pocket-size radio and a year later renamed itself Sony (*sonus* is Latin for sound). The Sony name remains prominent on all of its products. In 1960 Sony produced the first transistor TV in the world.

Increasingly, the world was Sony's market. (Great decision: Look to the world.) Its combination of smaller and smaller products at the leading edge of technology proved irresistible. In 1961 Sony Corporation of America was the first Japanese company to be listed on Wall Street, and in 1989, Sony bought Columbia Pictures. By 1991 it had more foreigners on its 135,000-person payroll than Japanese.

Morita became famous as the acceptable face of Japanese industry. Sophisticated and entrepreneurial, he did not fit the Western stereotype. (He also advocated a more assertive Japanese approach, in *The Japan That Can Say No*, which he coauthored with Japanese politician Ishihara Shintaro.)

Morita and Sony's gift was to invent new markets. Describing what he called Sony's "pioneer spirit," Morita said: "Sony is a pioneer and never intends to follow others. Through progress, Sony wants to serve the whole world. It shall be always a seeker of the unknown .... Sony has a principle of respecting and encouraging one's ability ... and always tries to bring out the best in a person. This is the vital force of Sony." While companies such as Matsushita were inspired followers, Sony set the pace with product after product, innovation after innovation.

Sony brought the world the handheld video camera, the first home video recorder, and the floppy disk. Its most famous success was the brainchild of Morita, the Walkman. The evolution of this now ubiquitous product is the stuff of corporate legend. Morita noticed that young people liked listening to music wherever they went. His decision was to seek a simple way for people to listen to music while they walked. He put two and two together and designed the Walkman. "I do not believe that any amount of market research could have told us that it would have been successful," he said, adding: "The public does not know what is possible, we do."

Such brilliant marketing design was no mere accident. "If you go through life convinced that your way is always best, all the new ideas in the world will pass you by," says Morita, who argues that analysis and education do not necessarily get you to the best business decisions. "You can be totally rational with a machine. But if you work with people, sometimes logic has to take a back seat to understanding," he says.

THE GREATEST LESSONS

Practice management with responsibility. Apart from his marketing prowess, Morita emphasized the cultural differences in Japanese attitudes toward work. "Never break another man's rice bowl," he advises, and observes: "Japanese people tend to be much better adjusted to the notion of work, any kind of work, as honorable." Management is regarded by Morita as where the buck stops and starts: "If we face a recession, we should not lay off employees; the company should sacrifice a profit. It's management's risk and management's responsibility. Employees are not guilty; why should they suffer?"

Start with a philosophy. Morita and Sony's story parallels the rebirth of Japan as an industrial power. "We in the free world can do great things. We proved it in Japan by changing the image of 'made in Japan' from something shoddy to something fine," says Morita. It cannot be forgotten that when Sony was first attempting to make inroads into Western markets, Japanese products were sneered at as being of the lowest quality. Surmounting that obstacle was a substantial business achievement.

Trust your nose. Morita's legacy of responsible management backed by imaginative marketing continues. Echoing the company creator's philosophy, the current president of Sony Corp, Nobuyuki Idei, says: "Right now, you don't need to be an engineer. You have to have a nose, and if you don't you can't run a company like Sony."

Forget market research. Morita had no need for market research; he knew there was a market for the Walkman. A similarly great decision that flew in the face of market research was made when Ted Turner launched the Cable News Network in 1980. No one thought a 24-hour news network would work. It did.

Great Decision #25

In the 1870s, doctors in Hartford, Connecticut decided to install the latest technology: the telephone. When there was a railroad accident nearby, the doctors were notified by telephone and were on the scene quickly. The event proved that the telephone worked: Skepticism gave way to enthusiasm.

In the nineteenth century, telephone technology was in its very infancy. It was in March 1876 that Alexander Graham Bell spilled acid on his trousers and bellowed for help. His assistant heard his cry over what was then called the audiotelegraph.

The trouble was that, having come up with a workable prototype, interest was limited. Indeed, the head of Western Union dismissed Bell's prototype as "an electrical toy." Western Union didn't buy Bell's patent (a subject of repeated dispute in later years).

Up against the telephone was the telegraph. By the 1870s, telegraph wires crisscrossed the world. The United States had over 200,000 miles of wire and 8,500 telegraph offices. The telegraph was entrenched and powerful; the telephone was strange and mysterious.

Two decisions removed the mystery from telephones. First, Bell and his business backers decided to market the telephone as a more personal tool. They emphasized the fact that the telephone enabled people to talk to each other. The conversation became a powerful result of the telephone. Rather than focusing on the technology, Bell and his colleagues focused on the result—the person-to-person connection.

The second great decision was more prosaic. All inventions need a few believers at the very start. The telephone's faithful were to be found in Hartford, Connecticut. Doctors in Hartford had seen the usefulness of the new device and many of them had installed telephones. Then in January 1878, there was a train crash at nearby Tarriffville. Someone at the local drugstore immediately telephoned the doctors, and they were on the scene quickly. The telephone proved its worth as a lifesaver.

The media highlighted the story, and the rest is history. By 1890, the telephone network covered New England. Then, through the 1890s, it spread to Chicago, Minnesota, and south to Texas. By 1904, North America was covered with telephone lines.

THE GREATEST LESSONS

Innovations need believers.   Once there is a groundswell of supporters behind an invention, it is difficult to stop. The attraction in having a mobile phone or being on the Internet is directly related to how many other people also have mobile phones or are on the Internet. The person with a mobile phone in hand is the greatest ad for mobile phone use.

Prove the value.   The telephone floundered in the face of skepticism until it was proved that it was patently useful to people. If a product proves its value, it is halfway to success. The typewriter underwent a similarly slow start. By 1880 only 5,000 typewriters had been sold. People couldn't see why they needed one when they could read and write quite effectively as it was. Then the business benefits of the typewriter were seen. Between 1880 and 1886, ten times as many typewriters were sold as between 1874 and 1880.

Great Decision #26

Honda arrived in the United States in 1959 to launch its big motorbikes. Customers weren't keen on the problematical performance of the big bikes, but admired the little Supercub bikes Honda's managers used. Honda decided to change direction and market its smaller bikes. It transformed the motorbike business virtually overnight.

In 1959, the Japanese motorcycle company, Honda, created the American Honda Motor Co. It was the company's first foray into the U.S. market dominated by Harley-Davidson, the British companies BSA, Triumph, and Norton, and the Italian manufacturer Motto-Guzzi.

At the time, Japanese products were still regarded with suspicion. Generally they were seen as inferior, as cheap imitations of the real thing. So the hopes for Honda's success in the United States appeared fairly forlorn.

Honda decided to launch its bikes in Los Angeles, as part of a grand strategy to sell into the United States. Its headquarters was at 4077 Pico Boulevard. Honda sent two of its executives to California, expecting to promote its larger bikes. Honda believed that its 250 cc and 350 cc models were the most suitable for the American market. The trouble was that these machines were unreliable and had oil leaks and clutch problems.

In order to get around town, the Honda salespeople used some of the newly developed 50cc bikes. These attracted a lot of attention wherever they went. Eventually the sales team received inquiries, not from motorcycle dealers, but from sports shops and other retailers. It seemed that fewer people were interested in the large machines, and against all of Honda's expectations, the 50cc bikes were to become the biggest seller.

Honda's crucial decision, therefore, was to change tack and start promoting the smaller machines, with the slogan, "You meet the nicest people on a Honda." This effectively opened up the U.S. market to Honda. New motorcycle owners flocked to Honda. In the 1960s 65 percent of its buyers were buying a motorcycle for the first time. Within four years Honda was marketing almost 50 percent of all motorcycles sold in the United States. By 1974, Honda had sold over 10 million Honda 50s.

THE GREATEST LESSONS

Learn, don't criticize.   The Honda team in America was not called back to Tokyo for failing to sell big motor bikes in the United States. Instead the company decided that if everyone wanted the small machines, that's what it would sell. Here was an organization that had put a lot of effort into a strategy for selling a product in a major market. A variety of alternative actions might have been taken: The salespeople could have been fired for incompetence because they failed to sell the big bikes; a new sales strategy involving more or different advertising for the big bikes could have been adopted. Many organizations would have been loath to let go of their marketing strategy, especially on account of a few comparatively junior people several thousand miles away, in a market that had not yet proved itself.

Never underestimate the competition.   Western attitudes toward Honda were complacent in the extreme. Traditional Western motorbike makers overlooked two crucial stats: In 1960 Honda employed 700 people in its research team, while its competitors averaged around 100; Honda's production per person-year was 159 units in 1962, a figure Harley-Davidson didn't reach until 1974.

Notes

[1] Quoted in Huey, J., "Eisner explains everything," *Fortune*, 17 April 1995.

[2] Vries, M. Kets de, and Dick, R., *Branson's Virgin: The Coming of Age of a Counter-Cultural Enterprise*, INSEAD, 1995.

[3] Quoted in Jackson, T. and Gowers, A., "Big enough to make mistakes," *Financial Times*, December 21, 1995.

[4] Hodgson, Phil, *What Do High Performance Managers Do?*, FT/Pitman, 1995.

[5] Parikh, Jagdish, *Intuition*, Blackwell, 1996.

LEADING BY EXAMPLE

Great decisions are not simply financial. They are not only personal. The greatest decisions have an ethical element.

Japanese empire creator Konosuke Matsushita advocated business with a conscience. This was manifested in his paternalistic employment practices. During a recession early in its life, the company did not lay off any people. This cemented their loyalty. "It's not enough to work conscientiously. No matter what kind of job, you should think of yourself as being completely in charge of and responsible for your own work," Matsushita said, going on to describe how he approached his work: "Big things and little things are my job. Middle-level arrangements can be delegated." He explained the role of the leader in a descriptive style. "The tail trails the head. If the head moves fast, the tail will keep up the same pace. If the head is sluggish, the tail will droop."

Great Decision #27

In 1995 Aaron Feuerstein of Malden Mills decided to keep the business open after a major fire in its factory. He kept the workforce of 2,400 people on the payroll, using his own personal savings.

Malden Mills was already a pretty unusual company prior to December 11, 1995. In an age of diminishing loyalty and relentless downsizing, it stood for traditional corporate values. Loyal employees worked alongside trusting management. Customer retention and employee retention both registered a staggering 95 percent. The company, based in Lawrence, Massachusetts, had remained steadfastly—some said foolishly—loyal to its home base. Founded in 1906, it moved to Lawrence in 1956 rather than follow its competitors and many more textile companies in their migration to the South.

Malden Mills stayed stoically put. Its loyalty seemed misplaced when, in the early 1970s, it made a disastrous move into fake fur. By 1980 the company was in Chapter 11 bankruptcy. Malden Mills struck back with the development of Polartec, a lightweight fleece that proved more successful—and more palatable—than fake fur. By 1995 sales of Polartec had reached $400 million.

Then a fire ripped through the company's factories, leaving more than a dozen people hospitalized and the company, it seemed, in ruins.

Malden Mills chief Aaron Feuerstein, the grandson of the company's founder, immediately announced that even with no production capacity and no immediate hope of producing anything, he would continue to pay the company's 2,400 employees and pay their healthcare insurance. It was estimated that paying the company's employees for 90 days and their healthcare for 180 days cost Feuerstein $10 million.

"I would nominate the decision by Aaron Feuerstein of Malden Mills in 1995 to keep his business open in the wake of a major fire that destroyed most of his company," says Charles Manz. "Most people would've been happy at their seventieth birthday to take the insurance money and go to Florida, but I don't want to do that," Feuerstein said. His decision appeared to be bad business at the time, even though it was highly moral.

In the end, Malden Mills was back to virtually full capacity within 90 days. A total of $15 million was invested in a new infrastructure. The committed and grateful workforce performed so well that productivity and quality shot up. Before the fire, 6 to 7 percent of the company's production was "off quality"; that number was reduced to 2 percent after the fire. Feuerstein said the company's employees paid him back nearly tenfold.

THE GREATEST LESSONS

Ethics come naturally or not at all.   Feuerstein considered his decision the natural thing to do. "Fifty years ago it would have been considered very natural for a CEO, if his plant burned down, to rebuild it and to worry about his people," he lamented.

Ethics pay.   Feuerstein's act was one of loyalty, honesty, and morality. But it brought paybacks; President Clinton was among those paying homage to Feuerstein by inviting him to Washington. "I always thought that perhaps in the long run [my employees] would return to me a quality product that would make Malden Mills continue to excel. But I never dreamed there would be any short-term advantage," Feuerstein said.

Businesses live with communities and vice versa.   Only Gordon Gekko would believe that companies and communities can be clinically separated. "One of the great lessons I learned these past few months is how fundamental our businesses are to the survival and health of our communities," said Feuerstein.

Great Decision #28

Two classics from Levi-Strauss cemented its reputation for ethical behavior. First, in 1906, an earthquake followed by a fire destroyed the company's headquarters and two factories; the company extended credit to its wholesale customers so they could get back on their feet and back in business. Then, during the Great Depression, CEO Walter Haas Sr. kept employees working by having them lay new floors at the company's Valencia Street plant in San Francisco, rather than laying them off.

Put on your blue jeans and there is a strong chance it will be a pair of Levi's. In the 1970s, disenchanted young Russians yearned for a pair of Levi's. They were a black market item in Poland and the Czech Republic. Levi's symbolized the freedom of the highway and the individualism of the West. They were James Dean's uniform. The Marlboro cowboy appeared to wear little else. Levi's remain icons—you know when you have arrived when a colorful and expensive coffee table book portraying your role in American culture is published—and a $100 million ad budget makes sure we don't forget that.

Thanks to its icon status, Levi-Strauss & Co is the world's largest apparel company, with revenues of $6 billion (1997). "Next time you're in a Shanghai launderette, or a juke joint in Joliet, or a boardroom in midtown Manhattan, look for us. We'll be a simple, but essential, part of someone's individual style," runs one company ad.

Not only is Levi's a top-ranking global brand, it has gotten there the ethical way. The company has consistently won awards from public bodies and praise from business leaders for its commitment to ethics, values, and social responsibility. In a poll of U.S. business leaders, Levi-Strauss was voted the country's most ethical private company, an honor shared with the Merck Corporation, consistently recognized as America's most ethical public company.

At Levi-Strauss, ethics and values are not afterthoughts or concepts tacked onto the business only after economic success is guaranteed. They are at the core of its culture and are perceived to be key drivers of business success. The company manages its ethics and values commitments with the same degree of care and attention that it devotes to other critical business issues. Like Marks & Spencer in Britain, Robert Bosch in Germany, and Tata Industries in India, the company's commitment to good ethics and values was set by its founding family. It has successfully transferred the family's personal commitment to ethics, values, and social responsibility into its worldwide business ethos and management practices.

The importance of that historical commitment cannot be underestimated. A culture of ethics, values, and social responsibility is built over time rather than overnight. Just as the Watsons influenced the culture of IBM, so the Haas and Koshland families have influenced the ethics and values of Levi-Strauss. The company has been a family-owned business for most of its 140-year history, and that has been critical in shaping its sense of values and its brand.

The original Levi Strauss (1829–1902) came from Bavaria. He arrived in New York in 1847 and worked with his half-brothers in their dry goods business. In 1853 Strauss went to San Francisco to set up his own business. His big break came when one of his customers, a Nevada tailor named Jacob Davis, showed him an idea he had for riveting men's trousers. The result was robust and long-lasting, suitable if you were a gold prospector or a farmer. Davis needed $68 to file a patent for the design. In 1873 Strauss and Davis patented the riveted trousers, or "waist-high overalls" as they were then called. The company prospered. When he died, Levi Strauss's estate was worth the colossal amount of $6 million.

The first major challenge faced by the company occurred in 1906, when an earthquake followed by a fire destroyed the company's headquarters and two factories. In response, Levi-Strauss extended credit to its wholesale customers so they could get back on their feet and back in business. The company continued paying its employees, and a temporary office and showroom were opened to give them some work to do while new headquarters and a factory were built.

A similar example was followed by the company during the Great Depression. Then-CEO Walter Haas Sr. kept employees working by having them lay new floors at the company's Valencia Street plant in San Francisco, rather than laying them off. Later, the company ensured equal employment opportunities for African Americans in its factories during the 1950s and 1960s, when it was expanding into the southern states. As the business grew, the community involvement tradition developed alongside. Levi-Strauss now draws over 40 percent of its revenues from its international businesses and manufactures products in over 50 countries worldwide. A quarter of its employees work outside of the United States.

THE GREATEST LESSONS

Trust has to be earned.   Standards have to be maintained. In the 1960s Levi's reached international markets and became accepted as youth-wear; the next decade was a different story. In the 1970s Levi's was successfully prosecuted under antitrust laws in California. In 1971 the company went public, which proved highly unsuccessful. It also brought in a CEO from Playtex who encouraged brand extensions. Levi's swimwear, Levi's headgear, and Levi's rainwear were among diversions from the main business that are best forgotten.

Between 1980 and 1984, the company's net income fell by over 80 percent. It shut or sold one-quarter of its U.S. factories and cut its workforce by 15,000—nearly a third. "The trust in the company and its leadership in particular was shattered," reflected the man charged with rebuilding it, Robert D. Haas, the great-great-grandnephew of the founder. He took over as CEO in 1984 and has successfully transformed the company's benevolent paternalism into a more dynamic, modern approach to managing ethics and values, one that engages employees in the process.

Pronounce what you stand for.   Ethics remain an integral part of Levi-Strauss's philosophy. The company published an Aspirations Statement in 1987 that challenges all employees to show leadership in "modeling new behaviors, empowerment, ethical management practices, and good communications." The Aspirations Statement also acknowledges that people deserve recognition for their work and positive behavior and commits the company to value and make good use of human diversity whether in age, race, sex, or ethnic group. It is not merely a decorative statement. Managers are not judged by economic performance alone. This sends a critical message about the importance of these values to the company. Up to 40 percent of management bonuses are decided on performance measures relating to ethics, values, and personal style in human relations as set out in the Aspirations Statement and elsewhere.

"We have told our people around the world what we value, and they will hold us accountable," says company president Peter Jacobi. "Once you do that, it's like letting the genie out of the bottle. You can't go back." Managers obviously like it; turnover among them at the company's San Francisco headquarters is a miniscule 1.5 percent annually.

Robert Haas has forcefully argued that an empowered workforce, one sharing the same values and aspirations for the company as managers and owners, will make a company a leader in the market. "You can't energize people or earn their support unless the organization has soul," says Haas. But, as recent results have proved, soul is no guarantee against the vicissitudes of business life.

Great Decision #29

In June 1894, Baron Pierre de Coubertin decided to convene an international conference in Paris. It led directly to the creation of the modern Olympic Games.

In the late nineteenth century, things moved at a slower pace than they do today. As a result, the story behind the creation of the modern Olympic Games covers a lengthy period. It was in 1889 that the first important decision in a trail of decisions was made, when the French government commissioned Pierre de Coubertin to report on the physical fitness of the nation's population and suggest methods to promote what it called "physical culture."

De Coubertin took three years to research the issue. He traveled widely and examined how other countries nurtured physical fitness among their people. "Everywhere I met discord and civil war had been established between the advocates of this or that form of exercise; this state of affairs seemed to be the result of an excessive specialization," he said. "The gymnasts showed bad will towards the rowers, the fencers towards the cyclists, the rifle marksmen towards the lawn-tennis players; peace did not even reign among the adepts of the same sports; the supporters of German gymnastics denied all merit to the Swedish and the rules of American football seemed to the English players not to make common sense."[1] He returned to present his findings at the Sorbonne on November 25, 1892. In his lecture, de Coubertin recommended that international sports competitions be held periodically. The seed of an idea was planted.

The idea reached the next stage in its life when de Coubertin convened an international conference in Paris. Here he suggested that a modern version of Ancient Greece's Olympic Games be created. It was decided that the event should be held every four years. The conference attracted attendees from 12 countries, and 21 other nations expressed an interest. A groundswell was emerging.

The conference led to the creation of the International Olympic Committee, with de Coubertin as General Secretary. In laying down the rules for the modern Olympics, the Committee made a number of important decisions. They decided that participants would compete regardless of race, color, creed, class, or politics and that there would be no financial prizes. "Olympism is not a system, it is a state of mind that can permeate a wide variety of modes of expression and no single race or era can claim a monopoly of it," said de Coubertin.

In 1896 the first modern Olympic Games were held in Athens. The ancient city had offered to be a permanent home for the Games, but the Committee, particularly de Coubertin, advocated that the Olympic Games be hosted by a different nation on each occasion. Forty thousand people came to watch the opening ceremony on April 6, 1896. De Coubertin expressed his hope that "my idea will unite all in an athletic brotherhood, in a peaceful event whose impact will, I hope, be of great significance."

THE GREATEST LESSONS

Move from vision to reality. The management lesson from the development of the Olympic Games is simply that visions can become reality.

Persist. Pierre de Coubertin's heart is buried at Olympia. His epitaph reads: "The main issue in life is not the victory but the fight. The essential is not to have won but to have fought well." Establishing the Olympic Games was a slow process, but de Coubertin stuck with his vision.

State your values up front. The Olympic ideal is based on simple values and precepts that were stated at the very start of the movement. They have lasted.

Great Decisions #30

During the Great Depression of the 1930s, American Express continued to cash its traveler's checks despite the fact that many U.S. banks were closed and their assets frozen. The American Express brand was more reliable than money.

The American Express Company began life as an express freight company. The company traces it origins back to 1851. It was created by the union of four express carriers—Wells & Co., Livingston & Fargo, Butterfield, and Wasson & Co.—and first operated under the slogan "Safety & dispatch," with a picture of a bulldog in its logo.

In 1882, as shipping large quantities of cash became increasingly hazardous, the company underwrote its first money order. The practice grew rapidly and American Express established relationships with a network of banks across Europe, building a business on the transfer of funds from the growing numbers of immigrants settling in America and sending money home to their families in Europe.

Its reputation for financial services was growing, but the company remained predominantly a freight delivery operation. That changed in 1891, with the issue of the American Express Traveler's Check, the first of its kind. This represented a major innovation: For the first time, the company was able to promise that a check written in dollars could be converted to a variety of other currencies. Best of all, it was automatically refundable if it was stolen or lost.

The arrival of the traveler's check freed the traveler to move across currency frontiers. The power of the traveler's check, however, resided in the power of the issuer's brand. This laid the foundations for the company's move into travel services. American Express began selling travel tickets for railroads and transatlantic ships.

When war broke out in 1914, 150,000 Americans found themselves trapped in Europe. Who could they turn to for help? American Express offices were besieged by panic-stricken U.S. citizens desperate to get home. The company rose to the occasion, posting money to points all across Europe. It is testament to the strength of its brand that in some countries, the locals preferred to trade in American Express traveler's checks rather than trust the local currency.

The company's reputation was boosted still further during the Great Depression of the 1930s, when the company continued to cash its traveler's checks despite the fact that many U.S. banks were closed and their assets frozen. The American Express brand was more reliable than money.

THE GREATEST LESSONS

Don't neglect branding.   American Express's branding put it ahead of the financial services industry. It was only at the beginning of the 1990s that the rest of the financial services world discovered branding. Despite American Express's patchy recent history, Interbrand, the London marketing group, claimed that it remains one of the true "super brands." In 1995, investment guru Warren Buffett took a 10 percent stake in the company, claiming that Wall Street's low valuation of the company's stock failed to take the power of the brand into account, a brand he called "synonymous with financial integrity and money substitutes around the world."

Back the right side.   During the American Civil War, the company served the winning side (always a great decision) and in the 1860s, transported vital supplies to Union army depots. Later it took part in the spread of democracy, issuing ballot papers to troops in the field. Always stay on the side of the customer.

Great Decision #31

In 1962 a young investor named Warren Buffett began buying shares in an ailing textile company called Berkshire Hathaway. The company now has a market capitalization of some $60 billion and Buffett is recognized as the greatest investor of our times. The moral element? A total of 99 percent of Buffett and his wife's net worth is in the company's shares.

Headquartered in Omaha, Nebraska, Berkshire Hathaway *is* Warren Buffett. The two are inextricably linked, both in corporate fact and in stock market mythology. The reality is that Berkshire Hathaway is no longer a humble textile company, but a corporate entity, a shell inhabited by 38,000 employees and made real by the passage of dollars to and from—but a shell with a market capitalization of about $60 billion.

In 1964 a share in Berkshire Hathaway Inc. was worth $19.46. By 1997, a Berkshire Hathaway share was worth nearly $25,488. These impressive figures have been widely quoted as Buffett's success has been examined from every angle. Yet if emulation is a measure of understanding, Buffett's approach appears little understood.

Above the maelstrom of analysts, commentators, and private investors stands Warren Buffett, a man of resolutely simple tastes who oozes old-fashioned decency from every pore. As he has become more famous and Berkshire Hathaway has become ever more successful, Buffett's public utterances and writings have become more playful. "As happens in Wall Street all too often, what the wise do in the beginning, fools do in the end," he wrote in 1989. This was followed in 1990 by: "Lethargy bordering on sloth remains the cornerstone of our investment style." He has cornered many a market, including the one in homespun wisdom.

Buffett advocates "focused investing." When gauging the wisdom of an investment, investors should look at five features: "The certainty with which the long-term economic characteristics of the business can be evaluated; the certainty with which management can be evaluated, both as to its ability to realize the full potential of the business and to wisely employ its cash flows; the certainty with which management can be counted on to channel the reward from the business to the shareholders rather than to itself; the purchase price of the business; the levels of taxation and inflation that will be experienced and that will determine the degree by which an investor's purchasing-power return is reduced from his gross return."[2]

Buffett admits that many will find such criteria "unbearably fuzzy." This is only partly the case. Analysis can lead to conclusions about the long-term economic prospects of a business. Analysis can also establish what is a reasonable purchase price and help predict future macroeconomic conditions that are likely to have an impact on the investment. But analysis falters and things begin to become fuzzy when we try to assess the incumbent management.

Buffett believes that executives should think and behave as owners of their businesses. He is critical, therefore, of the "indiscriminate use" of stock options for senior executives. "Managers actually apply a double standard to options," Buffett writes. "Nowhere in the business world are ten-year, fixed-price options on all or a portion of a business granted to outsiders. Ten months, in fact, would be regarded as extreme." Such long-term options, argues Buffett, "ignore the fact that retained earnings automatically build value and, second, ignore the carrying cost of capital."

Buffett is a ponderous minimalist in an age of hyperactive behemoths. He wrote, in 1933, "Charlie [Berkshire Hathaway's Vice Chairman, Charlie Munger] and I decided long ago that in an investment lifetime it's too hard to make hundreds of smart decisions.... Indeed, we'll now settle for one good idea a year. (Charlie says it's my turn.)" Buffett is humorously embarrassed by the purchase of a corporate jet: "It will not be long before Berkshire's entire net worth is consumed by its jet."

Perhaps the single most important aspect of Buffett's management style is that 99 percent of his and his wife's net worth is in the company's shares. "We want to make money only when our partners do and in exactly the same proportion," he explains to shareholders. "Moreover, when I do something dumb, I want you to be able to derive some solace from the fact that my financial suffering is proportional to yours." Warren Buffett's investment secret is revealed: Put all your eggs in one basket.

THE GREATEST LESSONS

Management counts.   Time and time again, Buffett returns to the issue of sound management. He lauds some of his own managers: "They love their businesses, they think like owners, and they exude integrity and ability." This is the quintessence of Buffett's philosophy: Given the right conditions, good managers produce good companies. Never invest in badly managed companies. "Charlie Munger, our vice chairman, and I really have only two jobs," says Buffett. "One is to attract and keep outstanding managers to run our various operations." The other is capital allocation.

The trouble is that there are a great many poor managers. "The supreme irony of business management is that it is far easier for an inadequate CEO to keep his job than it is for an inadequate subordinate," Buffett lamented in 1988, going on to criticize the comfortable conspiracies of too many boardrooms. "At board meetings, criticism of the CEO's performance is often viewed as the social equivalent of belching."

Keep it simple. Buffett's own management style is characteristically down to earth. "Charlie and I are the managing partners of Berkshire," he explained in 1996. "But we subcontract all of the heavy lifting in this business to the managers of our subsidiaries. In fact, we delegate almost to the point of abdication: Though Berkshire has about 33,000 employees, only 12 of these are at headquarters." In fashionable books this would be called empowerment; to Buffett it is simple common sense.

Admit your failures. Buffett admits to mistakes and errors in judgment. After a long struggle, Berkshire was eventually forced to close down its original textile company. "I should be faulted for not quitting sooner," Buffett told shareholders, going out of his way to praise the efforts of the management of the failed company as "every bit the equal of managers at our more profitable businesses." Even good managers cannot save what has become a bad business.

Great Decision #32

The New Coke fiasco of 1985 was one of the worst decisions on record. So, wherein lies the greatness? The decision to go back to the original recipe was brave and (relatively) speedy. We all screw up. The brave thing to do is to hold your hands up and admit it.

In 1984, executives at Coca-Cola were worried. The company appeared to be on the edge of a terrifying precipice. Its number-one place in the cola market appeared under genuine threat for the first time. Pepsi was catching up fast. Market share was slipping—Coca-Cola's market share lead was reduced to just less than 5 percent. Coca-Cola's ad spending was up, but it was having little effect. Pepsi had come up with a good ad play for a number two in the market: the Pepsi Challenge. The Challenge had led to a sharp increase in Pepsi's market share, up an immediate 8 percent. Trouble was, the Pepsi Challenge was more than a gimmick. In blind tests it seemed that drinkers actually did prefer Pepsi to Coca-Cola. This was not good news for the Coca-Cola marketing team.

Faced with these problems, Coca-Cola charged Sergio Zyman with responsibility for considering the previously unthinkable: changing the drink's recipe.

In September 1984 the Coca-Cola team came up with a recipe that, in blind tests, kept on winning. This, the company concluded, was the answer. Conveniently ignoring consistently negative market research about the possibility of changing the drink's formula, Coca-Cola went for it. On April 23, 1985, New Coke was introduced. On St. George's Day, the dragon came out to slay Pepsi.

New Coke, the company claimed, was smoother, sweeter, and preferable to the old version. This despite the fact that the old version was selling in many millions every day of the week. To call this the marketing faux pas of the century would be to understate the effect only slightly. Coke was faced with a barrage of criticism. On the other hand, its archrival Pepsi could barely contain its glee. Indeed, Pepsi quickly produced an advertising company that focused on the fact that "the real thing" remained unchanged.

Realizing that its move had been disastrous, Coke backtracked and, after 90 days, reintroduced the original coke. The recipe has not been tinkered with since.

THE GREATEST LESSONS

If it works, don't change it. There was more to Coca-Cola than the recipe. It stood for something. The company underestimated how strong that bond was.

Learn, don't blame. It was notable that the Coca-Cola top management team remained in place, and did so for a number of years. Heads did not roll. Indeed, Robert Goizueta, the CEO, received $1.7 million in salary and bonuses. The company's annual statement cited his "singular courage, wisdom and commitment in making certain decisions." (The reaction might have been different if the company had lost money. The company's stock actually reached an all-time high at the beginning of 1986.)

Great Decision #33

In 1982 Johnson & Johnson pulled Tylenol from store shelves. It put customer safety before corporate profit, and Johnson & Johnson CEO Jim Burke provided a lesson in corporate openness with the media.

The lack of truly great stories of ethical business behavior is amazing. In the quest for examples of ethical behavior, we tend to return time and time again to the classics. Perhaps the best-known of the classic examples is the case of Johnson & Johnson (J&J) and Tylenol.

In 1982, a psychopath put cyanide into some Tylenol capsules. Eight people died. In response, Johnson & Johnson withdrew the product—its entire inventory—from store shelves. A total of 31 million bottles were returned to J&J. It cost J&J $100 million. Then the company accepted responsibility—though it was clear that it hadn't actually done anything wrong.

J&J's response was candid. It opted for full cooperation with the media immediately. Later the company offered to exchange Tylenol capsules, which were the contaminated product, for Tylenol tablets. Many more millions of dollars were spent doing so.

Key to the company's response was the behavior of J&J CEO Jim Burke. The Irish-American emerged as an honest, straight-talking, highly responsible executive. He personally appeared on one TV program after another to take responsibility and keep people up to date on the situation. J&J's media response won plaudits. "What Johnson & Johnson executives have done is communicate the message that the company is candid, contrite and compassionate, committed to solving the murders and protecting the public," noted the *Washington Post*.

Tylenol remains one of the best-selling over-the-counter drugs. J&J invested heavily in restoring it to its previous position; it had 37 percent of the over-the-counter painkiller market. "It will take time, it will take money, and it will be very difficult; but we consider it a moral imperative, as well as good business, to restore Tylenol to its preeminent position," said Jim Burke. Thanks to the company's responsible handling of the situation, its sales recovered quickly.

THE GREATEST LESSONS

Write it down.   The fact that J&J had a Credo with clearly delineated standards of behavior made the crisis easier to handle. Burke had led a program to revisit the Credo and update it for the 1980s. This made the Credo a real and influential document that had a direct effect on people's behavior. Over a period of ten years, J&J had reconsidered the Credo. The Tylenol crisis brought its values into sharp relief. Instead of bringing in a contingency plan, the company carried on by expressing the principles and values included in the Credo. What the public saw was genuine, principled leadership.

React coolly and positively to a crisis.   Crises as awful as the Tylenol tampering rarely occur. J&J's decisive response met the challenge. It set up a crisis management team, identified the key people who needed to be involved, and limited the number of spokespersons. Most important of all, Burke took the lead.

Don't play it down.   When Perrier found traces of benzene in its products, it only recalled a small number from the North American market. The fallout from that perceived lack of a responsible reaction was far greater than the original problem.

Notes

[1] de Coubertin, Pierce, 1892.

[2] Cunningham, Lawrence, "The essays of Warren Buffett," *Cardozo Law Review*, 1997.

SUPERMODELS

The pursuit of the perfect means of organizing a business has taken managers through a bewildering array of decisions. New organizational forms emerge with regularity. Most are impractical or unworkable.

In the beginning there was hierarchy. A Greek named Dionysius the Aeropagite introduced the concept of hierarchy some 1,500 years ago. The word literally means "to rule through the sacred." Dionysius wrote that heaven was hierarchically organized. He also argued that this celestial structure had exactly nine levels: God was the CEO; the archangels acted as the top management team, and Jesus Christ was in a staff position to the right of God. According to the author of this theory, hell is also hierarchically organized, in nine layers. The entire structure is turned upside down, however, with purgatory as the prime motivator to "climb" the ladder.

Hierarchy continues its hold on organizational life. It is just a little different these days. Jack Welch of GE says that hierarchy is an organization with "its face toward the CEO and its ass toward the customer."

If organizations haven't been contemplating their hierarchical structure, they have in all likelihood been considering their size.

Throughout the twentieth century the predominant corporate myth was that big was good. From Henry Ford to Michael Eisner, Alfred P. Sloan to Jack Welch, size was considered all-important. Bravado of a particularly male kind has dominated. The current fashion for bigger and bigger mergers is just the latest manifestation of this obsession. We may accept that quantity is not quality in virtually every other area, but in business organizations the two remain hopelessly intertwined and confused.

The trouble is that expert after expert has pointed out that most people are not very creative in groups of 100,000, 10,000, 1,000, or even 500. People tend to be at their most creative in small teams. On the

Savannah Plain 200,000 years ago, it appears that clans had a maximum of around 150 members. Nigel Nicholson of the London Business School points to "the persistent strength of small to midsize family businesses throughout history. These companies, typically having no more than 150 members, remain the predominant model the world over, accounting for approximately 60 percent of all employment."[1]

The optimum size for a company is a matter of perennial debate. Virgin chief Richard Branson argues that 50 to 60 people is enough. "If a company gets too large, break it into smaller parts. Once people start not knowing the people in the building and it starts to become impersonal, it's time to break up a company," he says. Tom Peters suggests 150, and Bill Gates claims that around 200 is best. Nathan Myhrwold, the R&D manager at Microsoft, and John Allen, the man behind the artificial-world experiment Biosphere 2, both agree that eight people is about enough. Although the numbers vary, no one suggests that 215,000 employees is the optimum size.

Great Decision #34

In 1987 Percy Barnevik surprised commentators with the decision to create the world's largest cross-border merger, between Sweden's Asea and Switzerland's Brown Boveri. The $30 billion giant that resulted, Asea Brown Boveri, is now lauded as the organizational model for our times.

Asea Brown Boveri (ABB) is one of the most celebrated and most written about companies of our time. Case studies about the company abound. Those paying homage include Tom Peters, Sumantra Ghoshal, and Christopher Bartlett (authors of *The Individualized Corporation*), and virtually every other management thinker you care to mention. ABB is routinely decorated with corporate baubles as Europe's most admired company. Commentators praise; analysts purr.

First, the facts. Headquartered in Zurich, Switzerland, ABB is now the world's leading power engineering company, employing over 213,000 people in 50 countries. A $31 billion company, it is broken down into 35 business areas with 5,000 profit centers ("5,000 perceived companies," says chief executive officer Göran Lindahl).

ABB came about from the merger of the Swedish company Asea, then led by the redoubtable Percy Barnevik, and the Swiss company Brown Boveri. It was the biggest cross-border merger since Royal Dutch Shell's oily coupling. Barnevik became the CEO of the resulting ABB and revolutionized its organization and performance before he was succeeded by Lindahl in 1997.

Along the way, Barnevik has been portrayed as a kind of European Jack Welch. There are similarities. Both men have a long-held and passionate disdain for bureaucracy. Barnevik is famous for his 30 percent rule: When he takes over a company, 30 percent of headquarters staff are fired; 30 percent are moved to other companies in the group, and 30 percent are spun off into separate profit centers, leaving 10 percent to get on with the work. Both Barnevik and Welch are inveterate and powerful communicators who have managed to maintain a heady tempo of change. They have changed and then changed again.

While a great deal of attention has been paid to Barnevik's work as CEO, the story of the Asea Brown Boveri merger is a riveting one. Negotiations were conducted in secret. When the boards were shown the draft agreement for the first time, some directors had no idea a merger was afoot. They had an hour to read the papers. The entire process was extraordinarily quick. Due diligence was notable in its absence, as Barnevik pushed to clinch the deal. When a draft agreement was generated, Barnevik read it out line by line in front of both negotiating teams. Objections were ironed out on the spot. If voices weren't raised, it was taken as agreed. "We had to be fast; there could be no leakage; we could not have lawyers around; we had to trust each other," Barnevik reflected.

The merger was announced on August 10, 1987. The corporate world was stunned by its suddenness. The *Wall Street Journal* called it a merger "born of necessity, not of love." That comment overlooked the uncanny fit between the two companies. The merger was truly a marriage made in corporate heaven. Brown Boveri was international, Asea was not. Asea excelled at management, Brown Boveri did not. Technology, markets, and cultures fitted together. Of course, whether this was luck or strategic insight is a matter of continuing discussion.

Then, the decision having been made, Barnevik quite simply made it work. "The challenge set by Barnevik was to create—out of a group of 1,300 companies employing 210,000 people in 150 countries—a streamlined, entrepreneurial organization with as few management layers as possible," wrote authors Kevin Barham and Claudia Heimer in their book, *ABB: The Dancing Giant*. To enable this to happen, Barnevik introduced a complex matrix structure, what Lindahl has called "decentralization under central conditions." The company is run by an Executive Committee, with the organization below divided by business areas, company and profit centers, and country organizations. The aim is to reap the advantages of being a large organization while also enjoying the advantages of smallness.

ABB's matrix structure has been the source of much debate. It has been hailed as a new organizational model and Barnevik as GM's Alfred P. Sloan reincarnated. (Perhaps this is what GM had in mind when it appointed Barnevik a nonexecutive director.) Barnevik argues that the matrix system is simply a formal means of recording and understanding what happens informally in any large organization. The spider's web of the matrix is a fact of life.

Natural or not, the truth is that ABB's structure is complex, paradoxical, and ambiguous. As a corporate role model, ABB appears to be a nonstarter. ("I do not believe that you can mechanically copy what another company has done," advises Barnevik.) As a sophisticated means of managing this particular organization, ABB's structure has proven highly effective. What holds the company together is deep-rooted local presence, global vision, cross-border understanding, global values and principles for managing creative tension, global connection at the top, and global ethics. Putting that in place requires a CEO with the rare dynamism and intelligence of Barnevik. Imitators beware.

THE GREATEST LESSONS

Trust is all. The level of trust exhibited by the parties is perhaps the most striking thing about the ABB merger. Both sets of management recognized that it was a good idea. There was no political maneuvering. Secret discussions remained secret. Decisions were made and kept to. This atmosphere of mutual respect and trust was probably helped by the fact that it was a merger rather than a takeover. "A takeover would have destroyed a lot, psychologically, politically, and commercially," says Barnevik.

Treat people like mature adults. You could summarize ABB's management style and philosophy as management for and by grown-ups. It is seemingly free of infighting. Constructive debate is welcomed. Managers from different countries work together effectively. There is the impression that decisions are thought through, backed by analysis, then made and carried out with common support. ABB is a ringing endorsement for professional management at the end of the twentieth century.

Communication and clarity are critical components of leadership. Certainty, clarity and communication are the basic gifts of Percy Barnevik, the gifts he has liberally endowed ABB with. He possesses a rare certainty of judgment. He communicates constantly and brings absolute clarity to his decisions. The fact that Barnevik and ABB managed the succession of Göran Lindahl so adroitly and sensitively suggests that clarity and communication have become engrained in the corporate culture at ABB.

Great Decision #35

During the fifteenth century, the Incas expanded their empire. Their contribution to management was the realization that in any large, dispersed organization, communication and logistics are vital. As a result, they decided to create a network of administrative centers and warehouses for food, and to build thousands of miles of roads.

How do you run distant empires? It is an organizational challenge that has occupied minds for centuries—from the ancient Greeks and Romans to the CEOs of today's global corporations. One of the few civilizations to do it successfully was the Incan.

At their peak, the Incas controlled six million people spread over a huge area covering parts of modern Peru, Ecuador, Chile, Bolivia, and Argentina. They spoke many different languages and dialects. Deciding how to manage the people and their lands was a bit more problematical than contemplating how to manage a distant subsidiary.

The Incas had the advantage that force was an option, but their more peaceful means of persuasion were interesting preludes to later organizational behavior. The Incas decided on a highly standardized system of administration. Their system was based on units of ten and was the forerunner of the modern decimal system. To make sense of their lands they divided them into four quarters, or *suyus*, that met at the Inca capital, Cuzco.

The Incas also invested heavily in infrastructure. Their road system eventually covered over 23,000 km. The road system meant that the army could move quickly to sort out trouble and that goods could move equally speedily. All this was achieved at a time when the Incas had no vehicles with wheels.

The road system was combined with a highly complex logistical network. This was made up of way stations, imperial centers, forts, ceremonial centers, and other meeting and gathering points. Runners were specially trained to pass on messages. The system worked, but only briefly: The Inca empire functioned for only one hundred years.

THE GREATEST LESSONS

Logistics matter. Whatever kind of manager you are, speed of access is crucial. If you divide and rule, or manage by dictatorship, logistics are important: You have to put down insurrection with due speed. If you manage more humanely, logistics are even more important: Knowledge and experience must be shared and information communicated.

Some degree of standardization is essential. Allowing the proliferation of numerous systems and approaches usually results in unmanageable chaos.

Great Decision #36

Not many CEO appointments create a new corporate model. ITT's decision to appoint Harold Geneen in 1959 did just that. At that time the company had sales of $765 million; when Geneen retired in 1979, ITT had revenues of nearly $12 billion and was the largest conglomerate in the world. Geneen created a working model of rational, data-driven management.

Harold Geneen liked numbers. He loved numbers. His approach to business was the epitome of rationality. "The very fact that you go over the progression of those numbers week after week, month after month, means that you have strengthened your memory and your familiarity with them so that you retain in your mind a vivid composite picture of what is going on in your company," he said.

Harold Geneen (1910–1997) was a "'legendary conglomerateur" according to *BusinessWeek,* a relentlessly driven workaholic who believed that analytical rigor could—and surely would—conquer all.

Geneen allowed for no frivolity and, even in his late eighties, worked a ten-hour day at his office in New York's Waldorf-Astoria Hotel, running Gunther International, a company he bought into in 1992. Geneen combined hard work and an apparently slavish devotion to figures. "Putting deals together beats spending every day playing golf," he once said.

Geneen qualified as an accountant after studying at night school. He then began climbing the executive career ladder, working at American Can, Bell & Howell, Jones & Laughlin, and finally Raytheon, which was taken over by ITT. ITT had started life in 1920 as a Caribbean telephone company. Geneen joined the board of ITT in 1959 and set about turning the company into the world's greatest conglomerate.

Geneen's basic organizational philosophy was that diversification was a source of strength. There was nothing halfhearted in his pursuit of diversity. Under Geneen, ITT bought companies as addictively as Imelda Marcos once bought shoes. ITT's spending spree amounted to 350 companies and included Avis Rent-A-Car, Sheraton Hotels, Continental Baking, and Levitt & Sons, among many others. By 1970 ITT was composed of 400 separate companies operating in 70 countries.

The ragbag collection of companies was a managerial nightmare. To keep the growing array of companies in check, Geneen established a complex series of financial checks and targets, which he managed with intense vigor. Few other executives could have done so, but Geneen brought a unique single-mindedness to the task. As part of his formula, every month over 50 executives flew to Brussels to spend four days poring over the figures. "I want no surprises," announced Geneen. He hoped to make people "as predictable and controllable as the capital resources they must manage." While others would have watched as the deck of cards fell to the ground, Geneen kept adding more cards, while managing to be aware of the pressures and stresses each was under.

Facts were the lifeblood of the expanding ITT, and executives sweated blood in their pursuit. "The highest art of professional management requires the literal ability to *smell* a *real fact* from all others—and, moreover, to have the temerity, intellectual curiosity, guts and/or plain impoliteness, if necessary, to be sure that what you do have is indeed what we will call an *unshakeable fact*," said Geneen.

By sheer force of personality, Geneen made his approach work. (More cynically, you could say that ITT was a success within the parameters set by Geneen.) Between 1959 and 1977, ITT's sales went from $765 million to nearly $28 billion. Earnings went from $29 million to $562 million, and earnings per share rose from $1 to $4.20. Geneen stepped down as chief executive in 1977 and as chairman in 1979.

THE GREATEST LESSONS

A company built around the drive and energy of one man will not last longer than that man's career.   ITT rapidly disintegrated after Geneen's departure. Indeed, the writing was on the wall before that—the company's profits fell in 1974 and 1975. "Running a conglomerate requires working harder than most people want to work and taking more risks than most people want to take," said Geneen. His successors were unable to sustain his uniquely driven working style. The dark side of ITT was exposed: It had worked with the CIA in Chile and been involved in offering bribes. The deck of cards tumbled. In the month of Harold Geneen's death, ITT was taken over by Starwood Lodging.

Great Decision #37

While William Durant created General Motors, Alfred P. Sloan created the means by which it could be managed. Durant initially rejected Sloan's ideas. When Pierre Du Pont took control of the company in 1920, he decided to follow Sloan's planned reorganization. The dominant corporate form of the twentieth century (federal decentralization) emerged.

When Alfred P. Sloan took over the top job at General Motors, he inherited an organization that was ill-suited to achieve his aspirations. Ford had been able to achieve standardization and mass production by producing as narrow a product range as possible. Sloan wanted to produce a far greater range from a ragbag of companies; GM had been built up through the regular and apparently random acquisition of small companies. Sloan's conclusion was that through better running of the organization of the company, as opposed to the production line, his goal could be achieved. "Billy Durant created an unmanageable colossus, General Motors, but could not get it organized. One of his younger managers, Alfred P. Sloan Jr., proposed a reorganization, but Durant rejected it. When Durant lost control, Pierre Du Pont took over and liked Sloan's plan. This created a most modern form of organizing and propelled GM ahead of Ford in those early days of the industry," says Daniel Wren, author of *Management Innovators*.[2]

Sloan set about creating a coherent organization from his motley collection of companies. Central to his plan was his "organization study" which, said one observer, appeared to "have sprung entirely from his own head in 1919 and 1920." The study was an examination of the way the organization worked and reflected a new and novel idea. Sloan had a modest habit of suggesting that ideas just came to his mind. It should be noted that in virtually all cases, they didn't come to anyone else's mind.

As a result of his organization study, in the early 1920s Sloan organized the company into eight divisions—five car divisions and three component divisions. In the jargon invented 50 years later, they were actually strategic business units.

Each of the units was made responsible for all its commercial operations and had its own engineering, production, and sales departments, but was supervised by a central staff responsible for overall policy and finance. The operating units were semiautonomous, charged with maintaining market share and sustaining profitability in their particular area. In a particularly innovative move, Sloan directed the components divisions to sell products not only to other GM companies, but also to external companies.

The policy that Sloan labeled "federal decentralization" marked the invention of the decentralized, divisionalized organization. "Alfred Sloan did for the upper layers of management what Henry Ford did for the shop floor: he turned it into a reliable, efficient, machine-like process," observed *The Economist*. It should not be forgotten that Sloan was an engineer by training.

The multidivisional form enabled Sloan to utilize the company's size without making it cumbersome. "The multidivisional organization was perhaps the single most important administrative innovation that helped companies grow in size and diversity far beyond the limits of the functional organization it replaced," say contemporary thinkers Sumantra Ghoshal and Christopher Bartlett.

Sloan's innovation meant that executives had more time to concentrate on strategic issues, and that operational decisions were made by people on the front line rather than at a distant headquarters. It required a continuous balancing act, but it worked. By 1925, with its new organization and commitment to annual changes in its models, GM had overtaken Ford, which continued to persist with its faithful old Model T.

Although Sloan was lauded as a managerial hero by Alfred Chandler and Peter Drucker, the deficiencies of his model gradually became apparent. The decentralized structure built up by Sloan revolved around a reporting and committee infrastructure that eventually became unwieldy. As time went by, more and more committees were set up. Stringent targets and narrow measures of success stultified initiative. By the end of the 1960s, the delicate balance that Sloan had brilliantly maintained between centralization and decentralization was lost. Finance emerged as the dominant function, and GM became paralyzed by the organizational system that had once made it great.

THE GREATEST LESSONS

Structure requires flexibility.   The multidivisional form, say Christopher Bartlett and Sumantra Ghoshal, was handicapped by having "no process through which institutionalized wisdoms can be challenged, existing knowledge bases can be overturned, and the sources of the data can be reconfigured. In the absence of this challenge, these companies gradually become immobilized by conventional wisdoms that have ossified as sacred cows, and become constrained by outmoded knowledge and expertise that are out of touch with their rapidly changing realities."[3]

Size is an issue. It must be managed. "In practically all our activities we seem to suffer from the inertia resulting from our great size. There are so many people involved and it requires such a tremendous effort to put something new into effect that a new idea is likely to be considered insignificant in comparison with the effort that it takes to put it across ... . Sometimes I am almost forced to the conclusion that General Motors is so large and its inertia so great that it is impossible for us to be leaders," said Alfred P. Sloan.[4] How right he was.

Great Decision #38

In 1112, St. Bernard took charge of the Cistercian monastic order. He decided the situation was ripe for change and reorganization. This resulted in one of the prototypes of factory-style efficiency.

Religious organizations were *the* organizational models for many centuries. Think of the hierarchy of the Roman Catholic Church—low on layers but top-heavy on authority. (For a particular example of management Roman Catholic style, look at the Second Vatican Council [1962–65] convened by Pope John XXIII, which launched one of the biggest change management programs in history. It altered the shape of the Catholic Church into a decentralized, low-hierarchy management model that has stood the test of time.)

Or consider the decision to found the Society of Jesus (the Jesuits) in 1540 by Ignatius de Loyola. The Jesuits provided an organizational model with an emphasis on practical work rather than contemplation. The order became, according to Peter Drucker, "the most successful staff organization in the world."

Perhaps more obscure is the organizational inspiration of the Cistercians, part of the Benedictine order of monks. Established in 1098, their aim is to escape the excesses of worldliness and to live "remote from the habitation of man." The major disadvantage of this approach—especially in the eleventh century—is that when you are remote from humankind, you have to fend for yourselves.

Despite their faith, the Cistercians had a mixed record at fending for themselves. That is, until St. Bernard arrived in 1112 to take charge. St. Bernard (1090–1153) entered the Cistercian monastery of C'teaux and later became the first abbot of a new monastery at Clairvaux in Champagne.

St. Bernard provided dynamic leadership. He wrote exhaustively— 400 epistles, 340 sermons, various treatises, and a biography of St. Malachy. He decided that the order needed to become efficient in fending for itself, and founded more than 70 monasteries. As a result, the order embraced the latest in technology. Monasteries were remote from humans but they were near to streams. These were used to provide power (the waterwheel was a relatively recent but vital discovery), running water, and sewage disposal.

"These monasteries were, in reality, the best organized factories the world had ever seen," says John Lienhard of the University of Houston. "They were versatile and diversified."

THE GREATEST LESSONS

No organization is beyond change.   Even the most obscure, the most lazy, or the most inept organization can be shaken up and transformed— given inspirational leadership.

Technology is a force for good.   Monks would, you might think, be most likely to be skeptical about progress. St. Bernard convinced the Cistercians of the usefulness and godliness of progress.

Leaders communicate.   St. Bernard was a dynamic, driving force, even though he lived at a time when travel was arduous and communication torturously slow.

Great Decision #39

Michael Dell decided to sell PCs direct to consumers and built to order. Now everybody in the industry is trying to imitate Dell's strategy—too late.

Michael Dell's $12 billion inspiration was to bypass the dealer channel through which personal computers were then being sold. Instead, he decided to sell directly to customers and build products to order. Dell created a new channel for selling and manufacturing PCs. The new channel meant that the company wasn't hostage to the markups of resellers, nor was it burdened with large inventories. In fact, it was the ultimate in virtuous circles. Costs were low and profits high.

By using telephone sales and, more recently, the Internet, Dell bypasses the retailers to target corporate accounts utilizing dedicated, cross-functional account teams for large accounts and low-cost support staff for smaller accounts. Dell foresaw the growing sophistication and specific customer service needs of these accounts and the economic advantage of a direct model. Understanding the needs of a large number of individual accounts and tailoring products to meet their specific requirements can be accomplished not only more cheaply but more effectively without an intermediary. The result is mass customization, as opposed to the traditional method of broad market segmentation. After-sales support can be provided by corporate customers themselves, by Dell, or by a third party.

Dell's model not only cuts out the resellers; making PCs to order also greatly reduces working capital costs, and direct access to customers facilitates better product design, inventory management, and customer service.

Dell now has sales of $12.3 billion (1998) and is the world's number one direct-sales computer vendor. The company's Web site is expected to generate half of its transactions by the year 2000.

THE GREATEST LESSONS

Get close to customers.   When it's just you and the customer, "You actually get to have a relationship with the customer," says Michael Dell. "And that creates valuable information, which in turn allows us to leverage our relationships with both suppliers and customers. Couple that information with technology and you have the infrastructure to revolutionize the fundamental business models of major global companies." Direct knowledge of the end-consumer builds a satisfied customer base, increasing Dell's brand strength, lowering customer acquisition costs, and boosting customer loyalty.

Cut out the intermediaries.   Elimination of the retail channel saves on dealer margins. Dell reduced selling costs from 12 percent to only 4 to 6 percent of revenue. Feeding customer requirements directly into the production process shortens delivery lead times, and ready-to-boot systems mean quicker start-up times for buyers.

Great Decision #40

In 1931 Procter & Gamble introduced its brand management system that elevated brands to center stage and provided a blueprint for their management that has been followed ever since.

Procter & Gamble (P&G) launched Ivory Soap in 1879 and turned it into one of the world's first advertised brands. The company has been advertising and marketing itself ever since. Its annual ad spending is now in excess of $3 billion.

P&G has not only proved itself adept at marketing, it has also invented markets: Its Tide was the world's first heavy-duty synthetic detergent; Pampers created the disposable diaper business; and P&G can also lay claim to creating the two-in-one shampoo and conditioner business.

Perhaps P&G's greatest contribution to marketing came in 1931, when it took functional organization a stage further and created a new function: brand management. With brands like Ivory and Camay bath soaps, P&G believed that the best way to organize itself would be to give responsibility to a single individual: a brand manager. You can't argue with P&G's development since. Its revenues now near $40 billion annually.

The brand management system began to take shape in the 1920s, but it was not until 1931 that Neil McElroy, the company's Promotion Department Manager, created a marketing organization based on competing brands managed by dedicated groups of people. The system did not transform the world overnight, but gradually brand management became an accepted functional activity, an adjunct to sales and marketing—and often a fairly junior adjunct at that. Its popularity was fueled by the economic boom of the 1950s, which spawned a plethora of new products and brands. The selling of new brands was aided by the development of shopping centers and the emergence of television advertising. We had never had it so good and never had so much. Brand management provided some order amid the confusion introduced by prosperity.

By 1967, 84 percent of large manufacturers of consumer packaged goods in the United States had brand managers. Though the titles have changed, this system largely prevails today. It was only in the 1990s that the brand management system began to be challenged by trends such as reengineering, which sought to break down the long-established functional barriers.

Among those who cited P&G's development of brand management as a great decision was David Arnold of Harvard Business School. "Although the system is now under attack by some, it was an insight that spread like wildfire, lasted decades, and accelerated understanding of brands enormously," said Arnold, author of the *Handbook of Brand Management*.

THE GREATEST LESSONS

Manage everything.   Prior to the development of brand management, brands were left unattended at the corporate fringes. By introducing a systematic management approach, P&G proved that providing a framework can be very powerful and that inclusion is better than bemused or ad hoc exclusion.

Market everything.   P&G is a supreme marketing organization. Like Coca-Cola, it started early. In 1882 Harley Procter convinced his partners to allocate $11,000 to advertise Ivory Soap nationally for the first time. It was in 1896 that P&G's first color print ad—again for Ivory—appeared in *Cosmopolitan*. Advertising fueled growth; soon P&G was selling over 30 different types of soap, whose revenues funded continued innovation.

Great Decision #41

A virtual book store? It was a wild idea in 1994. Jeff Bezos had to choose between trying to create a truly virtual new organization or collecting his bonus. The decision was easy: The electronic commerce revolution was kick-started.

Jeff Bezos (born in 1963) has a 41 percent share in Amazon.com, which is reputed to be worth some $910 million. A Princeton graduate, he was the youngest vice president at Banker's Trust in New York. Then he made his break: "I tried to imagine being eighty years old, looking back on my life. I knew that I would hardly regret having missed the 1994 Wall Street bonus. But having missed being part of the Internet boom—that would have really hurt." Most people didn't even know the Internet boom was going to occur. Bezos did. How long this particular boom will continue is open to debate. For the moment, he remains an entrepreneurial model.

With 2.5 million books, Amazon.com is Earth's biggest bookstore. It is the exemplar of electronic commerce, and Bezos the recipient of many plaudits—though not, as yet, many profits.

Back in the electronic mists, the first books ordered through Amazon were dispatched in the fall of 1994 (personally packed by Bezos and his wife); in 1997 Amazon sold its one-millionth book. Sales in 1997 approached $148 million, an eightfold increase over the prior year. In 1998, sales grew 838 percent.

THE GREATEST LESSONS

Create informed dialogue with your customers. The original goal for Amazon.com was to provide the world's largest bookshop, but it quickly found that it was actually selling information as much as books. Today, for example, Amazon ("the toast of cyberspace" according to the *Financial Times*) sends customers an E-mail message every time a new book comes out on a subject in which they have registered an interest. That information also helps the company better understand its customers and target its marketing.

The site also encourages "chat" among its users as part of its service. To encourage discussion, it not only posts book reviews from leading newspapers, it also encourages customers to send in their own reviews, which are published on the Amazon site. This, say McKinsey consultants John Hagel and Arthur Armstrong in their book, *Net Gain,* is a powerful form of "community building"—a new trick for electronic channels and something that adds value to Web transactions.

Be patient.   Despite its popularity with consumers, business journalists, and academics, Amazon.com has yet to make a profit. Suggestions are that it is struggling with its new music format, and a host of imitators and competitors lurk. It may already be looking elsewhere; in 1998 Amazon bought Junglee Corp. and PlanetAll, two Internet companies.

The World's Ten Largest On-Line Bookstores in 1998

Bookstore Titles	Country	Deliverable (Million)
Amazon.com	United States	2.5
Alt.bookstore	United States	2.0
Abiszet Bucherservice	Germany	1.3
Foyles	United Kingdom	1.0
Barnes & Noble	United States	1.0
The Co-op Bookshop	Australia	1.0
Libro Web	Spain	1.0
Internet Bookshop IBS	United Kingdom	0.92
JF Lehmanns	Germany	0.75
Book Stacks Unlimited	United States	0.5

Notes

[1]Nicholson, Nigel, "How hardwired is human behavior?," *Harvard Business Review,* July-August 1998.

[2]Correspondence with author.

[3]Bartlett, Christopher and Ghoshal, Sumantra, *Managing Across Borders,* Harvard Business School Press, 1989.

[4]Sloan, Alfred P., *My Years with General Motors,* Doubleday, 1963.

GETTING ON

We all want to get on in life. The trouble is that we now have to manage our own careers. In the distant past, life unrolled before you. It was largely not yours to control. Then, during the twentieth century, the corporation emerged as the determiner of careers. Now, careers increasingly have to be managed by individuals. It is we, as individuals, who make the choices and call the shots.

The objective is simple enough. Happiness comes from working at what we are good at and in ways that suit our abilities. The trouble is that this combination rarely occurs. The reason, says Peter Drucker, is that we often have little idea of what we are good at. Ask yourself: What are my strengths? How do I perform? What are my values? Where do I belong? What should my contribution be?

The route to outstanding performance is to identify and improve your unique skills, and then to find jobs or assignments that match your skills, values, and so on. Ask questions, find the answers, and then you will be equipped to make the right decisions for your career—and life—development.

That's the modern advice, but if we look back, we can find a variety of tips on how to succeed. Herod the Great (73–74 BC) decided that if he wanted to get on in life, he needed to network. He did, first with Julius Caesar (Herod became CEO of Galilee), then with Marcus Antonius (Herod became King of Judea), and finally with Octavian, who kept Herod in the job. Herod was a Machiavellian corporate operator before either Machiavelli or the modern corporation.

Niccolo Machiavelli was a sixteenth-century Florentine diplomat whose career was a distinctly mixed bag. "The most influential business strategist ever born, Machiavelli was a useless businessman," said *Business Age* magazine.

123

Machiavelli portrayed business as a world of cunning, intrigue, and brutal opportunism. "I believe also that he will be successful who directs his actions according to the spirit of the time, and that he whose actions do not accord with the time will not be successful," he wrote. "Because men are seen, in affairs that lead to the end which every man has before him, namely, glory and riches, to get there by various methods; one with caution, another with haste; one by force, another by skill; one by patience, another by its opposite; and each one succeeds in reaching the goal by a different method." In other words, if it works, do it.

The second route to the top is that championed by motivational gurus through the ages—clean living, hard work, boundless energy, and excessive enthusiasm. This is the Dale Carnegie-Stephen Covey-Anthony Robbins school of success.

As with most things, there is a happy middle ground. Getting on in life and management does not necessitate either megalomania or hyper-activity. Sometimes, getting on involves making simple decisions that— usually inadvertently—trigger a chain of events. One thing can lead to another, but only if you do the right thing in the first place.

Great Decision #42

In the 1850s, Henry Dunant wanted to build a wheat mill in Algeria but couldn't obtain the land concession required to do so. In search of a document, Dunant decided to go the person at the top—in this case, Napoleon III. The result of his decision, after a long and winding road, was the creation of the Red Cross.

The simple symbol of the Red Cross remains one of the best known in the world. The reputation of the Red Cross is undimmed by the passage of time. In a cynical age, the Red Cross remains true to its original values in a way few if any organizations have managed to do. It is impartial, neutral, independent, and humanitarian.

There are now 160 Red Cross national societies, as well as the International Committee of the Red Cross and the International Federation of Red Cross and Red Crescent Societies. (Even its bewildering maze of bureaucracy fails to dim the power of the Red Cross name.) The Red Cross is truly global, in a way most commercial organizations can only dream of. Most countries have Red Cross societies; in Muslim countries they are called Red Crescent, and in Israel, Magen David Adom.

Happenstance and coincidence played a part in the development of the Red Cross. In the 1850s Henry Dunant (1828–1910) ran the Swiss colony of St. Étif in Algeria. He wanted to build a wheat mill, but couldn't obtain the land concession required to do so. In search of a document, Dunant decided to go the person at the top—in this case, Napoleon III.

Napoleon III was, at the time, fighting another battle, this time in northern Italy. Dunant set off to find him. Along the way, Dunant happened on the Battle of Solferino in Lombardy. It was a life-changing experience. Dunant spent days in the aftermath of the battle working to tend the wounded and save lives. He later wrote *A Memory of Solferino*, in which he wrote: "Would it not be possible, in time of peace and quiet, to form relief societies for the purpose of having care given to the wounded in wartime by zealous, devoted and thoroughly qualified volunteers?"

The answer was affirmative. On February 17, 1863 the International Committee of the Red Cross met for the first time. Its work, accurately mapped out by Dunant, continues to be carried out in the former Yugoslavia, Somalia, and Armenia. The American Red Cross alone gave $22 million to Rwandan refugees in Zaire.

THE GREATEST LESSONS

Go to the top. Don't go to the small fry; they will only pass the buck. Trek across the mountains to get to the CEO.

Stick with your values. The Red Cross's values are self-evident and remain identical to those mapped out by Dunant. Perhaps most importantly, they are continually reinforced by what is practiced in the field. Red Cross volunteers simply and bravely put the organization's values into practice. The values that support the brand are continually bolstered and reemphasized.

Think international. Globalization may be the corporate flavor of the month, but the truly great have long practiced and preached international perspectives and awareness. Great organizations and causes break down national barriers, because they do not consider them barriers.

Great Decision #43

During the fall of 1943, Paul Garrett of General Motors telephoned a young Austrian teacher and writer, Peter Drucker. Garrett invited Drucker to study GM, and the career of the century's foremost management thinker was launched.

Where would management have been without Peter Drucker? We can only imagine. What can be said is that management theory would have been an awful lot less interesting and, in all likelihood, less developed. Drucker (born in 1909) is the major management and business thinker of the twentieth century. Of that fact there is little dispute. "In a field packed with egomaniacs and snake-oil merchants, he remains a genuinely original thinker," observed the *Economist*. Prolific even in his eighties, Drucker's work is all-encompassing. There is little that executives do, think, or face that he has not written about.

Farsighted and always opinionated, Peter Drucker was born in Austria where his father, Adolph, was the chief economist in the Austrian civil service. (Freud had lectured in psychiatry to his mother.) Drucker's early experiences in the Austria of the 1920s and 1930s proved highly influential. "His background ... has done more than shape Mr. Drucker's style. It has left him with a burning sense of the importance of management. He believes that poor management helped to plunge the Europe of his youth into disaster, and he fears that the scope for poor management is growing larger, as organizations become ever more complicated and interdependent," noted the *Economist*. Drucker later worked as a journalist in London, before moving to America in 1937.

During the fall of 1943, Paul Garrett of General Motors called Drucker. It was a call placed apparently out of the blue. Garrett invited Drucker to study GM, and the career of the century's foremost management thinker was launched.

Drucker's resulting book, *Concept of the Corporation* (1946) was a groundbreaking examination of the intricate internal workings of General Motors and revealed the auto giant to be a labyrinthine social system rather than an economical machine. In the United Kingdom the book was retitled *Big Business* because, Drucker explains, "both Concept and Corporation [were] then considered vulgar Americanisms."

Drucker's books have emerged regularly ever since, and now total 29. Along the way he has coined phrases and championed concepts such as management by objectives. Many of his innovations have become accepted of managerial life. He has both celebrated huge organizations and anticipated their demise. (This has led to suggestions of inconsistency, though this is a rather hollow criticism of a career spanning more than 60 years.) His 1964 book, *Managing for Results,* was, Drucker says, the "first book ever on what we now call strategy"; *The Effective Executive* (1966) was "the first and still the only book on the behavior being a manger or executive requires."

Drucker's book production has been supplemented by a somewhat low-key career as an academic and sometime consultant. He was a professor of philosophy and politics at Bennington College from 1942 until 1949, and then became a professor of management at New York University in 1950—"The first person anywhere in the world to have such a title and to teach such a subject," he proudly recalls. Since 1971, Drucker has been a professor at Claremont Graduate School in California. He also lectures on Oriental art, has an abiding passion for the works of Jane Austen, and has written two novels (that were less successful than his management books). As if to prove that he is multidimensional, in his bio in *Who's Who* Drucker lists mountaineering as one of his recreations.

THE GREATEST LESSONS

Even great minds need a break.   If he hadn't received Garrett's phone call, Drucker may have followed a completely different career. Fortunately, the call sparked his interest.

Follow your interests, not the money.   Garrett's call aroused Drucker's curiosity. He has always followed its wandering routes. The genius of Drucker is that he has combined quantity and quality while plowing a thoroughly idiosyncratic furrow. He has resolutely pursued his own interests and the dictates of his considerable intellect, rather than the dictates of the dollar. In an age of thinkers as media personalities, Drucker refuses to be distracted. Disturbers of his California retreat receive a preprinted message assuring them that he "greatly appreciates your kind interest, but is unable to: contribute articles or forewords; comment on manuscripts or books; take part in panels and symposia; join committees or boards of any kind; answer questionnaires; give interviews; and appear on radio or television."

Remember what organizations are for.   GM was the first of many organizations to be analyzed by the great man. His conclusions were, and are, many and varied. They include pertinent observations on the nature of organizations: "Organization is not an end in itself, but a means to an end of business performance and business results. Organization structure is an indispensable means, and the wrong structure will seriously impair business performance and may even destroy it," wrote Drucker in *The Practice of Management,* Harper & Row, 1954. "The first question in discussing organization structure must be: What is our business and what should it be? Organization structure must be designed so as to make possible the attainment of the objectives of the business for five, ten, fifteen years hence."

Great Decision #44

The 1958 decision by Elvis Presley to join the army was brilliant career management. Overnight the rebel was repositioned as a mainstream hero. On his return in 1960, the crown prince became the king of rock and roll.

Elvis Presley graduated from high school in 1953. After that he worked as a truck driver and studied during the evenings to be an electrician. Later in 1953, he made a private recording for his mother at the Memphis Sound Studio. Proprietor Sam Phillips took more than his usual interest in the guitar-playing singer. In July 1954, Phillips, who was also owner of Sun Records, had Elvis back in the studio to record his first single, "That's All Right, Mama" and "Blue Moon of Kentucky."

The rest, as they say, is history. Local attention started a groundswell. Things moved fast. Elvis appeared on Jackie Gleason's *Stage Show* in 1955. He no longer harbored hopes of becoming an electrician. He made it big with his appearance in a 1956 TV show, Ed Sullivan's *Talk of the Town*. (Actually, only half of him made it big: His lower half was not shown when he performed.)

The million-selling "Heartbreak Hotel" and the movie *Love Me Tender* followed soon after. Then Elvis joined the army. Between 1958 and 1960, he was to be found in Germany and elsewhere as one of Uncle Sam's better-known foot soldiers.

Elvis could have avoided joining up. But he appeared to take the temporary absence from his meteoric rise philosophically. He served his time, and seeing him in his neatly pressed khaki uniform did wonders for the public's perception of Elvis. The shocking pelvic gyrations, the face that won over a million maidens simply with a smirk, and the rebel were swiftly forgotten. He was one of us, after all. It was okay to like him no matter who you were or how old you were. Elvis was mainstream.

THE GREATEST LESSONS

Career breaks can enhance employability. By putting his career on hold, Elvis and his manager Tom Parker actually fueled demand for the performer. People drank more during Prohibition; so it was with Elvis worship. On his return, Elvis became hugely popular. Movie followed movie and the hits kept coming.

But beware …   The downside of Elvis' career hiatus was that instead of picking up new skills, he picked up a few bad habits (such as the use of amphetamines).

Great Decision #45

In April 1978, McKinsey's John Larson decided to ask colleague Tom Peters to step in at the last minute to make a presentation on some research he'd done. The presentation led to In Search of Excellence, *the book that changed the business book market and created the management guru industry.*

Just before Easter of 1978, John Larson of McKinsey's San Francisco office had a problem. A computer crash meant that the material destined to be presented to a McKinsey client, Dart, wasn't available. Larson had to find someone to step into the breach and give a presentation to satisfy the client.

Larson called in another consultant, Tom Peters, who had been carrying out research into international best practice. Peters had traveled the world and had a stack of interview notes and a pile of tapes to prove it. Larson instructed him to put it all together in a presentation and to give it a sexy title.

One week later, on Good Friday 1978, Tom Peters gave his presentation to the Dart Corporation in Los Angeles. It was the birth of a management phenomenon that swept the business world and also elevated one of its parents into the pantheon of management gurus. Peters now fills auditoriums in countries as far apart as New Zealand and Belgium. Tom Peters has spawned an industry—the management guru business—populated by an array of top academics and consultants, a sprinkling of former executives, and a fair share of charlatans. Competition is fierce and the pace is fast. The world's managers demand a constant stream of books, seminars, conferences, and videos. They want more. Ideas are packaged and repackaged. Names become brands and every grain of innovative thinking is exploited for all it's worth. In this business, the bitchiness of academia is combined with the ruthlessness of the world of management consultancy.

For Peters, the presentation in Los Angeles in 1978 was the turning point of his career and his life. In his search for a sexy title, Peters came up with excellence. "The Dart presentation was called excellence—I've no idea why I called it that. It was about ideas that worked. It got a great response. That's the actual birth of excellence."

The process began in the spring of 1977, when Peters left his base at McKinsey's San Francisco office and traveled the world, visiting 12 business schools and a number of companies in the United States and Europe. Somewhat surprisingly, given that Japan was the emerging industrial powerhouse, his first port of call was Scandinavia.

After concluding his round the world jaunt in the summer of 1977, Peters was speedily dispatched to Copenhagen to present his findings to the McKinsey powers that be.

And that appeared to be that. Peters' conclusions remained vague and inconclusive. For the remainder of 1977, Peters carried on with his normal assignments. His filing cabinet bulged with the material he had collected on his travels, but it gathered dust until the Dart presentation came along.

Eventually, Peters and Robert Waterman developed a manuscript based on the material. At this point, the book was called *The Secrets of Excellence.* Honed and polished, the manuscript was delivered to the New York offices of Harper & Row in March of 1982. Harper & Row printed the dust jacket as the book was put through its final editing. Then, at a McKinsey meeting late in the summer of 1982, the subject of the book came up. McKinsey's founding father, Marvin Bower, intervened and said the title had to be changed, because it sounded as if Peters and Waterman were giving away the secrets of McKinsey's clients. It was a decision guaranteed not to please the publishers or the authors. But at McKinsey, Bower's word was usually final. The only other title contender was "Management by Walking Around," which was rejected. "In the end we came up with *In Search of Excellence,* but I've no idea where the idea came from," Peters says. Excellence was born.

THE GREATEST LESSONS

Go with the flow.   Peters went along with the evolution of the project and emerged, blinking into the sunlight, with a best-seller.

Dull assignments can lead to bigger things.   The Dart presentation was an act born of desperation. Larson's solution was inspired—he knew there was something in Peters' stuff—but undeniably desperate. It was an all too real compromise in the face of pressing reality.

Great Decision #46

Napoleon made some rash moves (Russia in winter, for example) but he was also the first leader to create a meritocracy, recognizing that competency was more important than breeding. His great decision was to promote people based on merit.

Napoleon Bonaparte has had bad press. This is a pity, and is mainly due to his astounding success. One of his most important insights was that talent is no respecter of birth. Careers should, he said, be "open to talents without distinction of birth or fortune." Napoleon recruited and promoted on the grounds of ability rather than nobility. As a child of the middle classes, he wasn't about to elevate noble lords above their ability.

This gave Napoleon a crucial advantage in battle. His opponents inevitably based their selection strategies on nobility. Their armies were led by dukes and lords rather than by talented professional soldiers. "Bonaparte judged men by what they could do, and not by their genealogy. He looked not at the decorations that adorned the breast, but at the deeds that stamped the warrior—not at the learning that made the perfect tactician, but the real practical force that wrought out great achievements," wrote J.T. Headley in his nineteenth-century study of the pocket general.

Napoleon's surest colleagues had risen from the ranks or were plucked from obscurity. One was the son of a grocer, another of a mechanic, and so on. "Wealth is a misfortune, primogeniture a relic of barbarism, celibacy a reprehensible practice," said Napoleon (failing to go on to explain the link among the three).

THE GREATEST LESSONS

Talent rules. Those who select and recruit by any other yardstick than talent are playing a dangerous game. Interestingly, another major decision involved much the same realization: Mutsuhito (1852–1912), emperor of Japan from 1869 to 1912, set that country on the road to modernization and industrialization through his decision to abolish the hereditary class system and import Western technological knowledge.

Understand motivation.   Napoleon understood motivation in a way that few, if any, of his contemporaries did. He knew which carrots to dangle—"You manage men with toys," he said of the Legion of Honor—and when to use the stick.

COMPETITIVE ADVANTAGES

Competitiveness guru Michael Porter argues that "in any industry, whether it is domestic or international or produces a product or a service, the rules of competition are embodied in five competitive forces." These five competitive forces are:

- **The entry of new competitors.** New competitors necessitate some competitive response, which will inevitably use some of your resources, thus reducing profits.
- **The threat of substitutes.** If there are viable alternatives to your product or service in the marketplace, the prices you can charge will be limited.
- **The bargaining power of buyers.** If customers have bargaining power, they will use it. This will reduce profit margins and, as a result, affect profitability.
- **The bargaining power of suppliers.** Given power over you, suppliers will increase their prices and adversely affect your profitability.
- **The rivalry among existing competitors.** Competition leads to the need to invest in marketing, R&D, or price reductions, which will reduce your profits.

"The collective strength of these five competitive forces determines the ability of firms in an industry to earn, on average, rates of return on investment in excess of the cost of capital. The strength of the five forces varies from industry to industry, and can change as an industry evolves," Porter says.[1]

Theories are neat; reality is messy. What can be said for sure is that competitive advantages are usually short-lived and can generally be divided into three groups: those created by being cheaper than the competition, those created by being better than the competition, and those created by being quicker than the competition.

Competitive advantages sometimes just happen. After Warner Brothers produced the first talkie in 1927, others joined the fray. But studios weren't soundproofed, so filming took time. RKO's number two executive, Sam Jaffee, suggested RKO should film at night, when it was quiet. It did so and stole a march on its rivals.

The only surefire rule is that competitive advantages change. Yesterday's competitive advantage is history. H-P chief Lew Platt has suggested that H-P should stand for "healthy paranoia," and explained why: "General Motors, Sears, International Business Machines were the greatest companies in their industries, the best of the best in the world. These companies did not make gigantic mistakes. They were not led by stupid, inept people. The only real mistake they made was to keep doing what it was that had made them successful for a little too long."

The hope that keeps many companies going—and many consulting firms in business—is that competitive advantage can be bought. Sometimes it can. Perennial losers, the Green Bay Packers brought in a team of consultants in 1991 to study how they could recapture the golden years. The consultants delivered their report; on plan, the Packers delivered Super Bowl XXXI. Life's like that sometimes.

Great Decision #47

After wreaking havoc in the 1980s and earning the nickname Neutron Jack, Jack Welch had reduced GE's workforce substantially and cut costs. What next? Welch decided to involve people as never before, through Work-Out.

By the end of the 1980s, GE was a leaner and fitter organization after a healthy dose of downsizing instigated by Jack Welch. Any complacency that may have existed in the company had been eradicated. In retrospect, Welch's greatest decision may have been to go in with all guns blazing. Dramatic though relatively short-lived change was preferable to incremental change in Welch's eyes. "Shun the incremental and go for the leap," is Welch's advice. No half measures for him.

Having proved that he could tear the company apart, Welch had to move onto the second stage: rebuilding a company fit for the twenty-first century. The hardware had been taken care of. Now came the software.

Central to this task was the concept of Work-Out, which was launched in 1989. This came about, it is reputed, after a chance question was asked by Professor Kirby Warren of Columbia University. Warren asked Welch: "Now that you have gotten so many people out of the organization, when are you going to get some of the work out?"[2] At this point 100,000 people had left GE. Welch liked the idea of getting the work out. With typical gusto, Welch brought in 20 or so business school professors and consultants to help turn the emergent concept into reality. Welch has called Work-Out "a relentless, endless companywide search for a better way to do everything we do."

Work-Out was a communication tool that offered GE employees a dramatic opportunity to change their working lives. "The idea was to hold a three-day, informal town meeting with 40 to 100 employees from all ranks of GE. The boss kicked things off by reviewing the business and laying out the agenda, then he or she left. The employees broke into groups, and aided by a facilitator, attacked separate parts of the problem," explains Janet Lowe in *Jack Welch Speaks*. "At the end, the boss returned to hear the proposed solutions. The boss had only three options: The idea could be accepted on the spot; rejected on the spot; or more information could be requested. If the boss asked for more information, he had to name a team and set a deadline for making a decision."[3]

Work-Out was astonishingly successful. It helped begin the process of rebuilding the bonds of trust between GE employees and management. It gave employees a channel through which they could talk about what concerned them at work and then actually change the way things were done. It broke down barriers. The gales of destruction were past. Creativity was in the air.

Welch the destroyer became Welch the empowerer. Work-Out was part of a systematic opening up of GE. Walls between departments and functions came tumbling down. Middle management layers had been stripped away in the 1980s. With Work-Out, Welch was enabling and encouraging GE people to talk to each other, work together, and share information and experiences. At first surprised, they soon reveled in the opportunity.

"In the early 1990s, after we had finished defining ourselves as a company of boundaryless people with a thirst for learning and a compulsion to share, it became unthinkable for any of us to tolerate—much less hire or promote—the tyrant, the turf defender, the autocrat, the big shot. They were simply yesterday," noted GE's 1997 Annual Report.

Work-Out worked. Back in 1981 when Jack Welch became its CEO, GE had total assets of $20 billion and revenues of $27.24 billion. Its earnings were $1.65 billion. With 440,00 employees worldwide, GE had a market value of $12 billion. By 1997, GE's total assets had mushroomed to $272.4 billion and total revenues to $79.18 billion. Around 260,000 employees, down a staggering 180,000, produced earnings of $7.3 billion and gave the company a market value of $200 billion.

Welch moved from arch destroyer and corporate enemy number one to potent creator. "The most acclaimed SOB of the last decade is the most acclaimed CEO of this one," announced *Industry Week* in 1994. The corporate demon king of the eighties was transformed into the role model for twenty-first century management. "The two greatest corporate leaders of this century are Alfred Sloan of General Motors and Jack Welch of GE. And Welch would be the greater of the two because he set a new, contemporary paradigm for the corporation that is the model for the twenty-first century," says the University of Michigan's Noel Tichy, a longtime observer of the Welch managerial style.

THE GREATEST LESSONS

Never stop.   Work-Out didn't bring Welch's revolution at GE to an end. The next stage was the introduction of a wide-ranging quality program. Entitled Six Sigma, it was launched at the end of 1995. "Six Sigma has spread like wildfire across the company, and it is transforming everything we do," the company reported two years later.

Invest in people.   People are the bread and butter of Jack Welch's managerial style. People matter—and are made to feel as though they matter. Says Welch: "We are betting everything on our people—empowering them, giving them resources, and getting out of their way."

Welch invests in people first by simply spending time with them. He calculates that he spends around half of his time with GE people, getting to know them, talking to them about their problems, and, yes, no doubt berating them if performance is down. It has been calculated that he knows around 1,000 people by name and has a good idea of their job responsibilities.

Jack Welch wants the best people. He wants to recruit them and retain them because it is good for his business. "The reality is, we simply cannot afford to field anything but teams of A players," he wrote in the company's 1997 Annual Report. "What is an A? At the leadership level, an A is a man or woman with a vision and the ability to articulate that vision to the team, so vividly and powerfully that it also becomes their vision. An A leader has enormous personal energy and, beyond that, the ability to energize others and draw out their best, usually on a global basis. An A leader has edge as well: the instinct and the courage to make the tough calls—decisively, but with fairness and absolute integrity."

Clearly, Welch wants people to perform. He insists that rewards packages be geared to individual as well as corporate achievements and ensures that rewards are carefully monitored and differentiated from business to business and from person to person. The message is that if you win, we all win. That's why 27,000 GE employees now have stock options.

Great Decision #48

Thomas Watson Jr. decided to commit IBM to the development of a new line of computers in 1962. He bet the company on the future: a big company and, as it turned out, a big future. The S/360s revolutionized the industry.

In recent years the reign of Thomas Watson Jr. (1914–1993) at IBM has gotten bad press. To some he was the son who inherited control of a corporate juggernaut and did little to put his own stamp on its destination. To others he was the man who brought IBM into the technological era and who mapped out how values and culture could shape an entire organization. In 1987 Watson was hailed by *Fortune* as "the most successful capitalist in history."

Whichever interpretation is correct, Watson had a significant role in the shaping of the modern IBM, a company whose trials and tribulations continue to fill the media. Watson Junior became chief executive in 1956 and retired in 1970. He then served as U.S. ambassador to Moscow until 1980.

Watson propelled IBM to the forefront of the technological and corporate revolution of the 1960s and 1970s. Most notably, Watson invested heavily in the development of System/360, which formed the basis of the company's success in the 1970s and 1980s. More money—$5 billion—was spent on developing the 360 than on the development of the nuclear bomb.

While the decision to go ahead with the 360 was brave and significant, Watson can also lay claim to another important decision: his decision to codify the IBM culture. Under Watson, the corporate culture and the company's values became all-important. They were the glue that kept a sprawling international operation under control. Watson created a blueprint for the modern corporation, circa 1960.

The three basic beliefs on which IBM was built were: Give full consideration to the individual employee; spend a lot of time making customers happy; and go the last mile to do things right. These had been established under Watson Sr., a man who knew all about customer service long before it was taken up by management gurus. But while Watson Sr. was content to drum the message home, his son took it a step further.

Watson Jr. codified and clarified what IBM stood for, most notably in his book, *A Business and Its Beliefs* (1963). The book outlined the company's central beliefs, or what would now be called core values.

Whether IBM collapsed (for a time) because it failed to change or because it failed to adapt its beliefs to new times is difficult to determine. Watson saw it coming. "I'm worried that IBM could become a big, inflexible organization which won't be able to change when the computer business goes through its next shift," Watson told Chris Argyris of Harvard in the 1950s, when Argyris did some work for the company. Watson saw the future but couldn't mobilize the corporate culture he did so much to clarify into the structures or practices that would enable IBM to pick up the baton.

THE GREATEST LESSONS

Even giants need to bet the company sometimes. The bets are just bigger.

Culture is a source of competitive advantage. Watson said that a culture could only be sustained by "a sound set of beliefs, on which it premises all its policies and actions. Next, I believe that the most important single factor in corporate success is faithful adherence to those beliefs. Beliefs must always come before policies, practices, and goals. The latter must always be altered if they are seen to violate fundamental beliefs."

Beliefs never change. Change everything else, but never the basic truths on which the company is based. "If an organization is to meet the challenges of a changing world, it must be prepared to change everything about itself except beliefs as it moves through corporate life. The only sacred cow in an organization should be its basic philosophy of doing business."

Great Decision #49

In 1987, Wal-Mart decided to move into the grocery business. In doing so, it changed the grocery industry and provided the foundations for its explosive growth throughout the 1990s.

In the late 1980s, Wal-Mart was eyeing Europe with increasing interest. Europe was experiencing a boom in hypermarkets. This format had been started by the European retailer Carrefour in 1962. By 1988 Carrefour ran 73 hypermarkets throughout Europe and, overall, there were 780. The idea behind hypermarkets was straightforward: The stores sold grocery and other general goods under one extremely large roof. Customers could load up with their week's groceries and buy clothes or household items at the same time.

Some U.S. chains already offered both groceries and general merchandise. The potential for Wal-Mart, the dominant general merchandise retailer, was clear. A combined merchandise and grocery operation offered the chance to continue the company's rapid expansion. At the time, Wal-Mart controlled 50 percent of the $150 billion discount store business. Another 32 percent of the industry was controlled by Kmart and Target. Any further inroads into market share were going to be difficult to achieve.

Grocery retailing, in contrast, was alluring. Wal-Mart saw that this $400 billion industry was extremely intriguing—and fragmented. The largest supermarket chain, Kroger, controlled a mere 6 percent of the market, and the top ten chains combined only mustered 19 percent of the market.

The downside of grocery retailing was simply that profit margins were low. Expansion was possible, but focused grocery outlets would always be handicapped by the industry's poor margins. Looking at the market differently, Wal-Mart saw a more positive message: Consumers visit grocery stores more regularly than general merchandise stores; if the opportunity was there for customers to cross the aisle and buy some general merchandise, the problems of low margins in the grocery business and intense competition in general merchandising could both be solved.

In 1987, Wal-Mart tested the waters with Hypermart USA. It brought in grocery experts and included a few grocery companies as partners. The experiment this culminated with the 1991 purchase of McLane & Co, a grocery and general merchandise wholesaler.

The first four Hypermarts provided a variety of lessons, which were all taken into consideration when Wal-Mart opened its first Supercenter in Washington, MO in March 1988. The new store was smaller than the Hypermart format. More stores followed. Over the next two years, five more Supercenters were built in Missouri, Oklahoma, and Arkansas. The smallest was 90,000 square feet; the biggest, 170,000.

With six Supercenters and four Hypermarts up and running, the piloting process was under way so that Wal-Mart could fully understand the business potential and the likely problems in introducing the combo format. One notable challenge was posed by inventory. Wal-Mart was used to carrying a full 60 days of inventory in general merchandising. In the grocery business, 25 days of inventory was normal, and fewer than 10 days for meat and other fresh produce. In response, Wal-Mart increased its inventory management capabilities and created manufacturing systems in certain areas.

It took four years of experimentation before Wal-Mart took the plunge into Supercenters. Between 1992 and 1998, it built 558 such stores. Rollout was rapid. Every single store incorporated on the lessons learned in the pilot phase of the early 1990s.

The end result is that Wal-Mart had 1998 grocery sales of $32 billion and is now the third largest supermarket operator, projected to become the largest by 2002. In 1999, Wal-Mart plans to open another 150 Supercenters, with 90 of them replacing existing discount stores. The mutually beneficial relationship between grocery and general merchandise has largely been confirmed. Superstores enjoy 30 percent higher general merchandise sales than their discount store counterparts.

Wal-Mart is now piloting another new format: Wal-Mart Neighborhood Markets, 40,000 square foot stand-alone supermarkets. Three have already been opened.

THE GREATEST LESSONS

Put your toes in the water, not your legs   Wal-Mart experimented and tried the Hypermarket format out in a limited number of locations. The stores were enormous (220,000 square feet), complex, costly, and made small profits, but they were important sources of learning. Most important, the company acted on what it learned from them.

Take control.   Why dilute your control by involving others? If you have the financial muscle, take control. Wal-Mart developed its own food distribution network rather than relying on other distributors. Its engineers and construction team learned from grocery store professionals to construct stores that were suitable to the new use and cheaper than those built by the competition. Test marketing continues even now, so that learning and improvement are ongoing.

Great Decision #50

Edward L. Bernays was the king of spin doctoring before it was a named phenomenon. His campaign to encourage women to smoke was a masterpiece. The high point was his decision to stage a march down Fifth Avenue with women brandishing their "torches of freedom." The march was, of course, led by Bernays' secretary.

The noble art of public relations is usually overlooked in surveys of great management practice. That's a pity, because it is a mine of good stories and masterly campaigns. The first king of spin could be said to have been Edward Bernays (1891–1995), who spun stories early in the twentieth century with practiced aplomb. As befitted a nephew of Sigmund Freud, Bernays was a master strategist.

Bernays was born in Vienna and arrived in the United States in 1892. He worked in propaganda during World War One and founded a public relations firm in 1919—the first in the country. Bernays described himself as a "counsel on public relations." He was reputedly still counseling when he was over 100 years old.

One of Bernays' classic campaigns was for the American Tobacco Company. The company wanted to encourage more women to smoke. Bernays launched a campaign that proclaimed the slimming benefits of cigarettes: Cigarettes were better than those nasty candies that piled on the pounds and, what's more, Bernays brought in "experts" to announce that cigarettes also acted as a disinfectant. If you wanted to be slim and healthy, smoking was a good thing.

At the time, the idea of women smoking in public places was frowned upon. It just wasn't acceptable for women to light up at the intermission in a theater or to stroll down the street smoking. Bernays suggested to any newspapers that would listen that this was a gross infringement of civil liberties. Smoking in public was promoted by him as an issue of emancipation. To ram the message home, he organized a march down Fifth Avenue of chain-smoking women. His secretary helpfully led the march. The results were immediate. There was a mountain of press coverage. The theaters in Broadway changed their rules; women could now use their smoking rooms.

"Bernays was one of the most interesting figures in the spin business at a buccaneering time," says the *Economist*. "American consumerism was taking off, there was plenty of demand for the services of public relations men and none of the tiresome modern restrictions on advertising that today make it harder to tell bald-faced lies."

Bernays and others of his kind laid the foundation for the modern PR merry-go-round. Bernays lived in more forgiving and less rigorous times, but his creative approach inspired many modern marketers.

THE GREATEST LESSONS

Every problem has a potentially imaginative and effective solution. "Let's start with the truth and work backwards," advises a contemporary master of spin.

Great Decision #51

Harvard Business School is the biggest name in business education because of educational excellence and more. Two decisions helped. In 1922 it decided to launch a journal, the Harvard Business Review, *that became a benchmark publication. In 1949, it set up the HBS Fund, provider of a large and growing source of finance. No other school can match this potent combo of branding, finance, and ivy.*

Harvard Business School was founded in 1908, and awarded its first master's degree in management in 1910. Although other schools, notably the Tuck School at Dartmouth, claim to have had graduate programs in management before that date, HBS was the first business school to require a university degree for entry to its management program.

What also set the school apart from the other business schools springing up in America at the time was the Harvard brand. The combination of the Ivy League prestige of Harvard University, the serious approach the new school took to the fledgling discipline of management, and its ability to attract gifted professors, some of them from other parts of the university, soon established the school as the top institution of its kind.

The branding was aided by the decision to publish a management theory publication. Wallace Donham, dean of Harvard Business School, oversaw the 1922 launch of the *Harvard Business Review*. The article on "The effect of hedging upon flour mill control" hardly set the pulse racing, but it was the beginning of a publishing success story and a prestigious addition to the Harvard brand. For more than 75 years the *Harvard Business Review* has been influential in shaping management thinking around the globe. Today, along with reprints of articles from the HBR archive, busy executives can buy audiotapes of articles to listen to in their cars or on airplane flights.

In addition, Harvard continues to churn out about 600 case studies a year (as well as around 40 books). In recent years, HBS branding has gone high-tech, creating CD-ROM and audio and video formats for many of its products. It is now possible to pay for HBR articles on-line and download them instantly. Even the traditional case study has taken a digital turn. Harvard put its first electronic case to work in 1996 and now boasts that its MBA curriculum is "virtually paperless," with an expanding number of electronic cases incorporating on-site video sequences and links to real-time information on the Internet.

The global reach of the *Harvard Business Review* means that Harvard's influence stretches around the world. The Indian Institute of Management, for example, was established with Harvard's support and remains a devout follower to this day. A number of European business schools also followed the Harvard model, including IESE, the prestigious Spanish school. In Asia, the Manila-based Asian Institute of Management was launched in 1968 and initially used material from Harvard for all of its programs. Harvard even offers a one-year program in applied economics at the Ho Chi Minh City Economics University in Vietnam (thus achieving by stealth what the United States failed to achieve through warfare).

The HBS brand is backed by an impressive money-raising operation. HBS has categories of donors so you know where you stand and, more importantly, how much others have given. The lowest rank is a participating donor (giving up to $249); donors progress up the scale: subscribing donor, supporting donor, sustainer, sponsor, patron, benefactor, leadership donor, leadership fellow, and finally, the hallowed ground of a leadership associate, donors who have made gifts of over $100,000. You can give to Harvard in any number of ways.

The sizeable HBS Fund was established in 1949 under the leadership of Frank L. Tucker (MBA, Class of 1930). Today the fund is headed by Thomas C. Theobald (MBA, Class of 1960), and a volunteer corps of 900 alumni. During the 1996-97 fund year, gifts and pledges exceeded $28 million, thanks to the generosity of over 12,000 donors who participated as part of their class reunion gift campaigns or annual giving. (This makes for an average donation of $2,333.) Approximately 31 percent of MBA alumni supported the HBS fund in 1997.

THE GREATEST LESSONS

Customer loyalty. Business schools tie their customers in. Alumni appear more willing to give donations to business schools—commercial ventures—than to universities, which are usually more needy. There is a self-perpetuating element to the matter of alumni fund raising. Alumni are almost obliged to continue to support their schools. Inverse blackmail is at work. After all, the value of an MBA lies in where you received it, rather than whether you studied global marketing in the second semester. By giving to your alma mater you are seeking to ensure that its standards remain high and that, as a result, your resume resounds with intellectual gravitas. If your resume boasts an MBA from a school that has since collapsed through lack of funds, its impact is lessened.

More cynically, some make donations as a statement of how wealthy they are and how seriously they take the education of the next generation. Having a successful businessperson's name attached to a building, room, chair, or program provides a constant message: Join this program and you may end up as rich and as wise as the person who endowed it. Of all the needy causes in the world, business schools would not place high on the list.

Great Decision #52

When he became CEO in 1993, Lou Gerstner decided not to split IBM, a move the previous CEO, John Akers, had prepared for. The company's revitalization owes a great deal to Gerstner's decision.

When he became CEO in 1993, former McKinsey consultant and turnaround master Lou Gerstner decided not to split IBM, even though this was a move the previous CEO, John Akers, had prepared for. "All or nothing" was Gerstner's refrain. Gerstner reflected that IBM had been through "an economic shock the equivalent of an earthquake"; another earthquake was the last thing it needed. Indeed, a vision was the last thing it needed. Nothing highfalutin'; just get on and manage was Gerstner's message.

Under Gerstner, IBM has made a surprisingly strong recovery. It has gotten back in touch with reality and with its existing and potential customers. Take its role in Internet development. In 1993, long-serving IBM exec John Patrick was arguing that everyone at the company should have their own E-mail address and that the company needed a Web site. "Connect with other people. If you become externally focused, you can change the whole company," said Patrick. It is interesting that Patrick's call to arms was basically a return to the company's first principles—get in touch with customers and communicate internally. The only difference was that Patrick was championing the use of the latest technology to do so.

As proof that IBM's culture has changed, forces were mobilized in a way the slow-moving monolith of the past never even contemplated. In 1995 only two of the company's 220,000 employees were working on Java. By 1997, 2,400 scientists and engineers throughout the world were doing so. Indeed, such is the cultural change that parts of IBM more resemble Microsoft. There is talk of breaking rules and using small eccentric groups to tackle problems from different angles, to bring fresh thinking.

Lou Gerstner stalks in the background, pulling the strings, exerting pressure when needed. In fact, his behavior appears to be a textbook example of modern leadership: empowering and coaching rather than controlling. At the same time, his feet appear firmly planted in commercial reality. Says Gerstner: "My view is you perpetuate success by continuing to run scared, not by looking back at what made you great, but looking forward at what is going to make you ungreat, so that you are constantly focusing on the challenges that keep you humble, hungry, and nimble."

Typically, when Gerstner was shown the Internet for the first time his reaction was, "This is great, this is a new channel for business. How do we make it real for customers? How do we make money on it?" The order of these priorities—first customers and then profit—is perhaps the vital lesson to be learned from IBM's renaissance and the rise, fall, and rise of the IBM brand.

THE GREATEST LESSONS

Get in touch with customers and with reality. IBM had grown distant from the marketplace. Gerstner reunited company and customer.

There's strength in togetherness. IBM could have been broken down into 100 significant organizations with 100 bright, new names. Gerstner's realization was that though this would have had some advantages, the continuing strength and resonance of the IBM brand name outweighed them.

Great Decision #53

In 1985, Rupert Murdoch decided to fund the building of a new printing plant in London that didn't require union labor. Computers were installed so that editorial content could be transferred directly to the page. On January 25, 1986, four million newspapers were produced at Wapping. Murdoch won the resulting war with the unions, changed the face of the newspaper industry, and launched his empire into the stratosphere.

In 1952 Rupert Murdoch inherited the *Adelaide News* and *Sunday Mail* from his father. *The Adelaide News*, as left by Sir Keith Murdoch, was an uninspiringly small newspaper. The Murdoch inheritance was no empire. To it, Rupert brought youthful vigor and a willingness to embrace the mass market.

Murdoch took to business life easily. His life had been a preparation for it. From the very start, Murdoch began stretching his wings. As the ink dried and the presses whirled, deals were struck. In 1960, Murdoch bought the *Sydney Daily Mirror* and tested the waters in the television market. Various deals came and went. Murdoch later explained the rationale behind his apparently indiscriminate purchasing: "We tended to take the sick newspapers, the ones that weren't worth much, that people thought were about to fold up." The purchases were backed by borrowing. Murdoch quickly learned that banks were only concerned about how reliably clients repaid their loans. Murdoch established a record of doing what he promised. Banks rolled over and offered more.

Perhaps the boldest sign of Murdoch's broadening ambitions was his founding of *The Australian*, the country's first national newspaper. Promising "to report the nation to Canberra and Canberra to the nation," *The Australian* started life in 1964. What set it apart from Murdoch's other ventures of the time was that it was a broadsheet with a heavier agenda (as well as a greater capacity to lose money). Firmly on its agenda was political power. *The Australian* placed Murdoch at the center of power. He became a national figure. Though the newspaper lost money for years (broadsheet equals unpopular in Murdoch's terminology), it made its mark.

By the late 1960s, Murdoch's Australian interests were many and varied. He began to look further afield. The first international deal that shaped the media image of Murdoch was the purchase of the British

Sunday newspaper, the *News of the World,* in 1969. The *News of the World* was downmarket and addictively populist long before Murdoch entered the newspaper business. It was not known as "the news of the screws" for nothing.

The *News of the World* was only the starter. It was a Sunday newspaper. The archaic inefficiency of Fleet Street meant that the presses remained silent during the week. It made obvious sense to use them.

And so, Murdoch rolled out a brash new form of populist journalism with the purchase for less than $780,000 of another British newspaper, *The Sun,* in 1969. To some *The Sun* was—and still is—the summation of all that is wrong with Murdoch. It is resolutely downmarket, famed for its page three topless models, pithy tastelessness, gung-ho nationalism, and insatiable interest in the comings and goings of the stars.

Thirty years later, *The Sun* and the *News of the World* remain highly lucrative parts of Murdoch's corporate empire, assembled under the News Corporation name. (In 1997 News Corp. reported that the *News of the World* had an average circulation of 4.5 million, while *The Sun* claimed to have over 10 million readers every single day.) Among Murdoch's other acquisitions was the *New York Post,* bought in 1976. His relationship with the *Post* has been a typically complex saga. He lost control of it in 1988—required to relinquish it by U.S. law because he bought a local TV station, WNYW—and regained control in 1993, when the newspaper was acquired once again by News Corp.

In 1981, Murdoch marked a remarkable new chapter in his career when he bought the *London Times,* fighting off bids from the newspaper's editor (William Rees-Mogg) and a group of journalists, as well as from the editor of the *Sunday Times,* Harold Evans, and Robert Maxwell. The "top people's paper" was an unlikely bedfellow for *The Sun.* Indeed, with its court circulars and overbearing sense of tradition, the *Times* was an unlikely bedfellow for any other newspaper. There were predictable gasps of amazement when Murdoch, the downmarket populist, bought the bastion of English journalism. There were various pronouncements of impending doom, and elderly clergy turned the pages with new excitement, anticipating the arrival of their very own page three girl.

The purchase of the *Times* marked another important threshold in Murdoch's career. It was, after all, the newspaper of the Establishment that Murdoch had expressed his distaste for. Murdoch found himself waging war on behalf of the Establishment.

Murdoch's newspapers in the U.K. were profitable, but with growing interests elsewhere, he was keen to maximize their profit potential. Cash cows have to be milked. Blocking his path were the outdated processes and unions of Fleet Street. Demarcations and closed shops meant that the unions had a stranglehold on how and where newspapers were produced. Proprietors had gone along with these arrangements for decades. (It should not be forgotten that they, too, were culpable for the resulting inefficiencies and extravagances.) Murdoch drove a bulldozer through them.

In Wapping, in the East of London, he built a new printing plant that didn't require union labor. Computers were installed so that editorial content could be transferred directly to the page. On January 25th, 1986, four million newspapers were produced at Wapping. War ensued.

Over the following months, Wapping became a battlefield. Thousands of picketers, from the print unions and others, attempted to bring printing at the plant to an end. The protests became increasingly violent and raged throughout most of 1996. The end result was complete victory for Murdoch. The printers were paid off with $96 million and disappeared into history. Murdoch was left with a much more efficient operation and substantially reduced costs. Valuations of News Corp. soared from $300 million to $1 billion.

Murdoch's confrontation with the unions was a defining moment in his career and in the history of the unions. It was also the defining moment in the public's perception of Murdoch. He was shown to be decisive and ruthless, someone who got what he wanted. He was clearly not only a powerful man but someone who was intent on using his power to create a business empire.

The end result for Murdoch is a personal wealth now calculated at many billions of dollars, from $3 billion to $10 billion depending on whom you believe. Murdoch's is a truly global empire; according to *Asia Week*, Murdoch is the fourth most powerful person in Asia. The total assets of News Corp. as of March 1998 were $33.2 billion, and the company had total annual revenues of $13 billion.[4] The News Corp. empire includes BSkyB, News International, the Los Angeles Dodgers, HarperCollins, 20th Century Fox, Fox TV, Star TV, and many more companies—more than 780 businesses in 52 countries. It is a huge global business empire that criss-crosses the earth.

THE GREATEST LESSONS

Move on.   During the 1980s, Murdoch created his empire. Acquisition followed acquisition. His aspirations appeared ever bolder. In 1985 he acquired Fox Studios; seven Metromedia TV stations followed in 1986; and, in 1988, he paid Walter Annenberg $3.2 billion for *TV Guide.*

Risk it all.   The spending flurry was impressive, but it was built on a mountain of debt that made Robert Maxwell appear the very model of financial prudence. The beginning of the 1990s marked a turning point. News Corp.'s fabulous debts, $7 billion and counting, nearly brought it to its knees. Only a last-minute deal at the beginning of 1991 saved Murdoch's empire from ignominious collapse.

Undaunted, Murdoch has refused to stand still. During the 1990s, Murdoch's ambitions have expanded. His deals have become more global and more distant from his newspaper roots.

Great Decision #54

*In 1992, clothing retailer Benetton had a turnover in excess of $1.6 billion
and appeared to have the world at its feet. Luciano Benetton recognized that
the company needed to embrace the future before it was too late. He decided
to invest $128 million in an advanced clothing factory. The company
changed the way it did business.*

The first inspired decision in the Benetton family was made in 1965,
when Giuliana Benetton decided to knit a brightly colored sweater.
Thirty years later, Giuliana and her three brothers have a global retail
chain of 7,000 stores in 120 countries, all selling brightly colored
sweaters. Giuliana controls the work of over 200 designers at Benetton's
Design Center. The company produces more than 200,000 garments a
day. Benetton is one of the most eye-catching brand arrivals of recent
decades. Its worldwide annual sales now total 2,871 billion lire (or $1.53
billion).

Benetton's success has been fueled by huge investments in logistics
and manufacturing that have lowered production costs and, more
importantly, allowed the company to be immediately receptive to
changes in the marketplace. This has proved highly important in moving
Benetton forward with the times.

For example, Benetton was outsourcing and contracting out work
long before those practices became fashionable. As long ago as 1982,
Benetton contracted work out to 200 units, of which the company
owned a mere 9.

"Benetton achieves a major advantage over its competition because
of its ability to 'micro-market' to individual retailers on a quick-
response, just-in-time basis," says marketing guru Philip Kotler.
"Benetton's logistical advantage results in much lower inventories and
warehousing costs, and its profits are 30 percent higher than the U.S.
apparel industry average. Benetton owes a large part of its success to its
high investment in information power."[5]

The most crucial decision in this area was made in 1992, when
Benetton had a turnover in excess of $1.6 billion and appeared to have
the world at its feet. At the time, Benetton was (according to the company) the third best-known brand in the world. But Luciano Benetton
wanted to move the company forward. At the company's headquarters in

Ponzano Veneto, a seventeenth-century villa just outside Castrette di Villorba, north of Venice, Benetton came up with a highly ambitious plan. In response to high labor costs, Benetton invested a massive $12.8 million in an advanced clothing factory. It installed state-of-the-art systems; software tells the machines what to make in response to information coming directly from the company's stores worldwide.

Its investment in technology has made Benetton's Castrette industrial complex among the world's most advanced. The factory produces almost 100 million garments every year. It includes an automatic distribution system that handles over 30,000 packages every day. This process is managed by only 19 people; a traditional system would require at least 400.

Benetton is now taking its brand to bigger and bigger stores. It has opened megastores in major European cities, and its U.S. flagship is the 1,200 square metre store in New York's Scribner Building on Fifth Avenue. Its support systems and studious awareness of how it is pushing and pulling its brand suggest that, in Benetton's case, bigger may well become better.

THE GREATEST LESSONS

Keep it simple.   Benetton's trademark products, colorful clothing, are strikingly simple but instantly recognizable as the company's. It has extended its interests with caution. Its other brands now include Zerotondo, Sisley, and 012. In 1997 it moved into sportswear and sporting equipment through such brands as Prince, Nordica, and Rollerblade.

Attract attention.   The "United Colors of Benetton" brand provides a large variety of easy options for advertising images. Eschewing them, Benetton has cornered the market in surprising, some would say offensive, advertising. One ad features Luciano Benetton naked except for the line, "I want my clothes back." Then there are the shocking images of people dying. Gratuitous? Perhaps it is, but it has largely succeeded in cementing Benetton's position as a colorful outsider.

Photographer Oliviero Toscani has been responsible for some of the most striking images used by Benetton. "Everything we do is about impulse, about guts," says Toscani. "That's what built Benetton; Luciano didn't test the market for a taste in colored sweaters." The ads are an expression of the brand, of the company, and of Luciano Benetton.

This is how the company explains the images it uses to sell more sweaters: "Benetton's communication strategy was born of the company's wish to produce images of global concern for its global customers.... Benetton believes that it is important for companies to take a stance in the real world instead of using their advertising budget to perpetuate the myth that they can make consumers happy through the mere purchase of their product." True enough, but Benetton's "stance" is often difficult to determine.

Change while you are ahead. Advice often given, rarely heeded.

Great Decision #55

In desolate postwar Japan, Toyota decided to listen to an obscure American statistician, W. Edwards Deming, who arrived unheralded in 1947. Deming introduced Toyota to quality techniques; Toyota conquered the world.

During the last four decades of the twentieth century, Western car makers lurched from one crisis to another. They were always a step behind, and the company they were following is the Japanese giant, Toyota.

When you enter the Toyota headquarters building in Japan, you find three portraits. One is of the company's founder; the next is of the company's current president; and the third is a portrait of the American quality guru, W. Edwards Deming.

In 1918 Sakichi Toyoda formed a company called the Toyoda Spinning & Weaving Co. In the 1930s the development of automatic looms convinced the company that its future lay elsewhere. Kiichiro Toyoda, the founder's son, had studied engineering and visited the United States and Europe. He decided the future was in car making and changed the company's name to Toyota in 1936. Kiichiro Toyoda remained as company president until 1950, and the company was run by a member of the Toyoda family until 1995.

The first Toyota car was the Model AA. (As something of an insurance policy, the company also continued its old business; looms were still produced until the early 1950s.) In the 1950s Toyota established offices in Taiwan and Saudi Arabia. It began making forklift trucks (and is now number one in the world in that market) and entered the American market (1958) and later the U.K. market (1965).

Toyota's initial foray into the U.S. market proved unsuccessful. Its Crown model was designed for the Japanese market and was ill-suited to American freeways. Eventually Toyota got it right. In 1968, the success of the Corolla enabled it to make a great leap forward. By 1975 Toyota had replaced Volkswagen as the United States' number one auto import. It got right into the heart of the American market in 1984, when Toyota entered into a joint venture with General Motors to build Toyotas in the United States. (The joint venture also makes the GM Prizm.)

More successes followed. The Camry was the best-selling car in the United States in 1997. Toyota is now developing its interests in hybrid electric cars; launched in Japan in 1997, they are projected to be rolled out globally in 2000. It is also involved in financial services, telecommunications and housing, marine engines and recreational boats, parts distribution and aviation services.

Toyota is now the third biggest car maker in the world (behind GM and Ford). It sells five million vehicles a year (1.3 million in North America, 2 million in Japan, and 0.5 million in Europe). In Japan it has nearly 40 percent of the market. Its 1998 sales were $88.5 billion, with a net income of $3.5 billion.

Behind Toyota's success is the presence of Deming and the practical application of his quality philosophy. Toyota's decision to follow Deming's quality philosophy was one of the most influential of the twentieth century. While Western companies produced gas-guzzling cars with costly, large, and unhappy workforces in the 1970s, Toyota was forging ahead with implementation of Deming's ideas. In the early 1980s, Western companies finally woke up and began to implement Deming's quality techniques. By then it was too late. Toyota had moved on. (In fact, it didn't mind telling Western companies all about total quality management for this very reason.)

Toyota progressed to what would become labeled "lean production," or the Toyota Production System. (The architect of this system is usually said to be Taichi Ohno, who wrote a short book on the Toyota approach and later became a consultant to the company.) From Toyota's point of view, there was nothing revolutionary in lean production. In fact, lean production was an integral part of Toyota's commitment to quality; its roots can be traced back to the 1950s and Deming's ideas. In 1984, when Toyota entered into a joint venture with General Motors in California, the West began to wake up and the word began to spread.

THE GREATEST LESSONS

Employ just-in-time production.   There is no point in producing cars, or anything else, in blind anticipation of someone buying them. Waste (*muda*) is bad. Production has to be closely tied to the market's requirements.

Quality is everyone's job.   Responsibility for quality rests with everyone, and any quality defects need to be rectified as soon as they are identified.

Look at the value stream.   Instead of seeing the company as a series of unrelated products and processes, view it as a continuous and uniform whole, a stream that includes suppliers as well as customers.

Lean works.   Toyota took Deming's ideas and moved them forward. In Toyota's hands, the ideas evolved. In contrast, Western companies tended to import them en masse. At Toyota, Deming's quality philosophy has been translated into lean production. "Lean production is a superior way for humans to make things," argue lean production gurus James Womack and Daniel Jones. They are right. If, as Toyota has largely done, you get it right, lean production provides the best of every world: the economies of scale of mass production; the sensitivity to market and customer needs usually associated with smaller companies; and the job enrichment that makes employees happy and productive.

The trouble is that getting it right has proved difficult. In many cases, Western organizations were so committed to their very different ways of working that the changes required were impossibly all-embracing. Companies cannot transform themselves overnight.

People matter.   The West continues to equate leanness with numbers. Lean production is seen as a way of squeezing more production from fewer people. This is a fundamental misunderstanding. Reduced numbers of employees are the end, rather than the means. Western companies have tended to reduce the number of employees and then declare themselves lean organizations. This overlooks all three of the concepts that underlie genuine lean production (just-in-time manufacturing; responsibility for quality; and viewing the company as a value stream). Womack argues that while lean production requires fewer people, the organization should then accelerate product development, to tap new markets and to keep the people at work.

Great Decision #56

Decide to cut out the extras and focus on what you can deliver and what the customer really wants. How many companies can truthfully say that they have made that decision? Herb Kelleher of Southwest Airlines can.

Over the course of 27 years, Southwest has stamped an indelible mark on the airline industry. Herb Kelleher has proved that differentiation is a CEO-level issue. "It is still the low-cost airline by which all others are judged," notes the *Financial Times*. Yet if you look at the basics, Southwest doesn't appear to have a lot going for it. Its product is, from a businessperson's perspective, plainly inferior. There is no first class, no seat assignment. These are things that matter to harried businesspeople anxious to finish a report on the laptop during the flight. Yet Southwest still captures a reasonable share of business traffic. Its services are high in frequency and punctual, and passengers have shorter ground journeys because Southwest flies to alternative airports. The value of higher certainty of flight time and shorter overall door-to-door time is immeasurable to many business travelers. The icing on the cake is the legendary, much talked about Southwest service, which is built around people enjoying their work and enjoying helping customers. Southwest started wooing customers (male ones, at least) with a Love theme (drinks were called Love Potions). Now, it does so through its promise of "positively outrageous service."

In a business that is often bland, Southwest sends out strong, simple messages to customers and employees that add value for both groups. The information flow combines to help the company's logistics. Turnaround times tend to be quicker than those of competitors, often by 20 minutes, because staff work together. Another win–win situation is the company's use of a standardized fleet of Boeing 737s. Using a single plane model means maintaining a single inventory of spare parts. Customers don't care if they fly a 737, so long as the plane gets them to their destinations safely and on time.

Kelleher's decision was not rocket science, but it gave Southwest a huge head start. The airline invented a new channel—low-thrills, low-cost, high-service flights—and, as a result, captured the Texas market and built up a tidy cash pile to expand into other plum markets such as California. Now the seventh biggest carrier in the United States, Southwest has a long record—24 years—of uninterrupted in-the-black performance. Others have boarded the bandwagon. United has attempted to "rise higher" and the latest no-thrills airline, Go, comes from British Airways. They have a lot of catching up to do.

THE GREATEST LESSONS

Keep it simple.   The only other airline exec who seems to have gotten Kelleher's message is Gordon Bethune, chairman and CEO of Continental Airlines. When he took on the job in 1994, it didn't appear to be the greatest career move. In fact, it appeared to be the career equivalent of suicide. Continental was in disastrously bad shape. The previous CEO, Frank Lorenzo, had followed a cheap fare strategy that had gotten the airline nowhere. It had been in Chapter 11 bankruptcy and seemed stuck in the red. Its market capitalization of $230 million was actually less than the trade-in value of its planes. (This must rank as one of the most inglorious achievements in recent managerial history.) Continental lost $204 million in 1994.

Things were bad. "We even had pilots turning down the air conditioning and slowing down planes to save the cost of fuel. They made passengers hot, mad, and late," says Bethune.

On arrival, Bethune took the double locks off the executive offices on the twentieth floor. He ordered that the planes be repainted so that they were all the same color. He instructed staff to ensure that the planes were cleaned three times more often than they had been. He announced that every month that Continental was in the top five airlines in on-time performance, everyone would get $65; the company lost $6 million per month by being late. In the first month Continental was seventh; in the second it was fourth, and in the third, first.

In 1996 Continental made profits of $556 million and its market capitalization is now $3 billion. *Fortune* selected it as the Most Improved Company of the 1990s. "We don't spend a lot of time on strategy; we spend more time on implementation, making sure we get it done," says Bethune who, like Herb Kelleher, has proved single-handedly that management is not aeronautic science: Great management is simple.

Great Decision #57

Miletus in Ancient Greece (around 500 BC) may have been the cradle of philosophy, but it was also keenly commercial. Its leaders decided to specialize in wool and associated products, thus setting the precedent for areas to be based around a particular industry. Miletus was a distant prototype of Silicon Valley.

It now appears natural for regions to specialize in certain types of activity. Knowledge and experience can be pooled, as can natural resources. Think of the Industrial Revolution in England and the cluster of textile companies in Lancashire and Yorkshire. Such was the level of specialization there that an entire town, Darwen in Lancashire, was dedicated to making loincloths for India. Of course, when the Indians started making their own loincloths, the town virtually ground to a halt overnight.

The decision made at Miletus in Ancient Greece (around 500 BC) to specialize in wool and associated products may have been one of the earliest examples of regional specialization. Now, of course, we have Silicon Valley, Silicon Glen, Silicon Fen, and various other regions identified with particular industries.

Harvard Business School researcher Michael Porter has examined the role of such areas in national competitiveness.[6] Porter's research initially covered ten countries: the United Kingdom, Denmark, Italy, Japan, Korea, Singapore, Sweden, Switzerland, the United States, and Germany (then West Germany). Porter has since extended his study to include India, Canada, New Zealand, Portugal, and the state of Massachusetts.

Porter sought to determine what makes a nation's firms and industries competitive in global markets and what propels a whole nation's economy to advance. "Why are firms based in a particular nation able to create and sustain competitive advantage against the world's best competitors in a particular field? And why is one nation often the home for so many of an industry's world leaders?" he asked. "Why is tiny Switzerland the home base for international leaders in pharmaceuticals, chocolate, and trading? Why are leaders in heavy trucks and mining equipment based in Sweden?"

Porter returned to first principles, but not to Miletus. "The principal economic goal of a nation is to produce a high and rising standard of living for its citizens. The ability to do so depends not on the amorphous notion of 'competitiveness' but on the productivity with which a nation's resources (labor and capital) are employed,'" he wrote. "Productivity is the prime determinant in the long run of a nation's standard of living."

Porter identified a central paradox, one that confirms the management wisdom of the ancient Greeks. Companies and industries have become globalized and more international in their scope and aspirations than ever before. This, on the surface at least, would appear to suggest that the nation has lost its role in the international success of its firms. "Companies, at first glance, seem to have transcended countries. Yet what I have learned in this study contradicts this conclusion," said Porter. "While globalization of competition might appear to make the nation less important, instead it seems to make it more so. With fewer impediments to trade to shelter uncompetitive domestic firms and industries, the home nation takes on growing significance because it is the source of the skills and technology that underpin competitive advantage."

Porter's conclusion was that it is the intensity of domestic competition that often fuels success on a global stage.

Applying Porter's theory, the decision made in Miletus would have been driven by factor conditions (these once would have included natural resources and plentiful supplies of labor; now they embrace data communications, university research, and the availability of scientists, engineers, or experts in a particular field); demand conditions (strong national demand for a product or service can give the industry a head start in global competition); related and supporting industries (industries that are strong in particular countries are often surrounded by successful related industries); and firm strategy, structure, and rivalry (domestic competition fuels growth and competitive strength).

THE GREATEST LESSONS

Sharing local expertise can be a source of competitive advantage. At one time, companies would have shared natural resources. Now, the sharing of infrastructures and knowledge networks can enable companies to be more successful.

Beware the danger of conformity.   The danger is that regional specialization can breed conformity and complacency. Moving to Palo Alto and setting up a company suffixed by .com does not make you an e-commerce entrepreneur, only a follower.

Great Decision #58

In the late 1960s, an unheralded British academic was invited to try out his theories in Belgium. That decision led to an upturn in the Belgian economy. The academic returned to obscurity, though his ideas live on in organizations as diverse as the African National Congress and GE.

"Unless your ideas are ridiculed by experts they are worth nothing," says the British academic Reg Revans, champion of a concept called action learning. "I've been talking about action learning for sixty years, but it's not me you should be talking to; talk to the people putting it into practice."[7]

Interest in Revans' ideas continues to pour in from all corners of the globe. The Pentagon is enthusiastic; the ANC has taken up action learning; Revans fields queries from Australia, Sweden, and many more countries. But in his homeland, he remains an outsider.

Part of the reason for Revans' isolation is cultural. While others seize upon action learning as a dynamic, commonsense way forward, the British appear particularly uncomfortable with the idea and its implications. As theories go, action learning is simple, even deceptively so. It is concerned with learning by doing, a process for which Revans created a simple equation: $L = P + Q$. Learning occurs through a combination of programmed knowledge (P) and the ability to ask insightful questions (Q). "The essence of action learning is to become better acquainted with the self by trying to observe what one may actually do, to trace the reasons for attempting it and the consequences of what one seemed to be doing," says Revans.

Action learning is the antithesis of the traditional approach to developing managers. Indeed, Revans' contempt is at its most withering when he considers business schools: "There are too many people concealing their ignorance under a veneer of knowledge. Instead of hiding our ignorance we should be bartering it." "Flatulent self-deception" is how Revans colorfully describes the neatly defined case studies that are the cornerstone of business school courses.

Though it runs against conventional educational wisdom, action learning's ancestry is ancient. Reg Revans peppers his papers and conversation with an array of inspirations, from Buddhism to the Bible. He can trace his personal advocacy of action learning back to the sinking of the *Titanic,* when he was nearing his fifth birthday. His father was a naval architect who was involved in the inquiry into the disaster. "He said to me years later that what the inquiry proved was that we must train people in such a way that they understand the difference between cleverness and wisdom. The education system, then and now, encourages cleverness."

The seed of a lifetime's fascination was sown and began to flourish in the 1920s, when Revans worked at Cambridge's Cavendish Laboratories alongside five Nobel Prize winners. In the quest to split the atom, the eminent scientists tended to champion their own particular fields. To break the logjam, physicist Lord Rutherford decided that the team should hold a meeting every week to discuss their difficulties and ask fresh questions. (This in itself was a great and far-reaching decision.) "Even though they had won Nobel Prizes, they were willing to acknowledge that things could be going on elsewhere. They asked questions," Revans remembers.

If leading thinkers could introduce humility and the sharing of knowledge into their working practices, why couldn't others? After the Second World War, Revans moved on to become the first director of education and training at the U.K.'s National Coal Board and set about applying his ideas. He concluded that colliery managers and miners themselves needed to acknowledge the problems they faced and then attempt to solve them.

With characteristic frankness, Revans announced that he saw no need to employ a team of specialist tutors. He then spent two years underground examining the real problems facing miners. This reinforced his idea that learning takes place when problems are aired and shared in small groups of "comrades in adversity." (In the 1990s, Nelson Mandela called it "grassroots collaboration.") The pits where workers tried Revans' methods recorded a 30 percent increase in productivity. Revans' approach was not well received by management, and he eventually resigned.

In the 1960s, Revans was apparently set on an academic career. The U.K.'s first professor of industrial administration at Manchester University, he was involved in the debate about the nature of the city's soon to be established business school. Again, action learning ruffled establishment feathers and Revans departed for Belgium, to lead an experiment launched by the Foundation Industrie-Université with the support of the country's leading businesspeople and five universities.

In Belgium Revans found more fertile ground. "Brussels had been selected as capital of the Common Market, much to everyone's surprise. They decided if they were to be the administrative center of Europe, they needed to develop international understanding." The Belgians responded to the idea of action learning with enthusiasm. Top managers were exchanged between organizations to work on each other's problems. "I wasn't there to teach anyone anything. We got people talking to each other, asking questions. People from the airline business talked to people from chemical companies. People shared knowledge and experience," Revans explains. With minimal attention from the rest of the world, the Belgian economy enjoyed a spectacular renaissance. During the 1970s, Belgian industrial productivity rose by 102 percent, compared with 28 percent in the U.K.

Yet again, Revans' success failed to cross the Channel. When his huge book, *Action Learning,* was published, he ended up buying most of the copies. Simple though it may seem, action learning provides a challenge that organizations have found too sizable even to contemplate. If learning revolves around questioning, there can be no assumption that managers know best purely because of their status. When the world was top down, Revans looked from the bottom up and saw a new world of possibilities.

Revans' ideas have been applied in rice growing in Bihar, among the isolated villages of Nigeria, in London hospitals, and in many other situations and organizations. There are some suggestions that action learning may be gaining in popularity. Jack Welch at GE is an adherent of a form of action learning. GE's Work-Out can be seen as a form of using action teams to tackle particular problems. This ad hoc approach carries the proviso that the teams do not necessarily understand what they have learned.

Indeed, many of the fashionable management ideas—teamworking, reengineering, the learning organization—contain elements of action learning. Revans is encouraged, but remains unconvinced: "What we need now is not a savior or a guru, but an active movement so that, no matter what their culture, people work together to understand local difficulties. I'm not saying this is the final answer. There is no final answer for anything."

THE GREATEST LESSONS

Ask questions. While programmed knowledge is one-dimensional and rigid, the ability to ask questions opens up other dimensions and is free-flowing. Revans argues that educational institutions remain fixated on programmed knowledge, instead of encouraging students to ask questions and roam widely around a subject.

Cross-fertilize ideas. "The ultimate power of a successful general staff lies not in the brilliance of its individual members, but in the cross-fertilization of its collective abilities," says Revans.

Great Decision #59

During the mid-thirteenth century, a number of cities in Northern Germany entered into an association to promote their commercial interests. The Hanseatic League eventually had about 40 members, with representatives throughout Europe.

Trade cartels are nothing new. They are proof that there really is strength in numbers. Partnerships in trade of varying shapes and sizes have been around since time immemorial. In 1072–1073, the Italian cities of Venice and Genoa entered into partnership to fund commercial voyages. The joint venture was born.

The Hanseatic League was perhaps the most powerful and longest-lasting trade group. The League's origins lie in the middle of the thirteenth century. Traders from throughout Flanders sent delegates to conduct negotiations on their behalf with Countess Margaretha.

The League, according to German academic Rainer Postel, "was neither a society nor a corporation; it owned no joint property, no joint till, no executive officials of its own; it was a tight alliance of many towns and communities to pursue their respective trading interests securely and profitably."

The League went through various permutations and machinations. A sign of its power came in 1358, when delegates from the Hanseatic towns held a meeting in Lübeck. They discussed violations of its rules in Flanders. The result was a trade embargo against Flanders, a crude commercial weapon still much in use today. This one worked.

The actual membership of the League remains somewhat confused. Calculations vary, ranging from 70 to 200 members. Members were towns in the Baltic area of northern Europe including modern-day Germany, Belgium, and Sweden.

The Hanseatic League reached its peak in the fifteenth century. Decline set in as towns and regions were annexed or fought among themselves. By 1669, only six towns turned up at the Hanseatic League meeting.

THE GREATEST LESSONS

None of us is as strong or as smart as all of us.   The Hanseatic League provided a blueprint for trade alliances that followed. Its central belief in shared knowledge and resources was sound.

Teamworking is ridden with complexity.   The Hanseatic experience also demonstrates the human capacity for dispute and lack of accord.

Notes

[1]Porter, Michael, *Competitive Strategy,* Free Press, 1980.

[2]Vicere, Albert, and Fulmer, Robert, *Leadership by Design*, Harvard Business School Press, 1998.

[3]Lowe, Janet, *Jack Welch Speaks*, John Wiley, 1998.

[4]Despite its global reach, News Corp. has quite legally mastered the art of minimizing its tax liabilities. One calculation estimated that News Corp., the umbrella corporation, paid a meager 1.2 percent tax on profits between 1985 and 1995.

[5]Kotler, Philip, *Marketing Management*, Prentice Hall, 1994.

[6]Porter, Michael, *The Competitive Advantage of Nations*, Macmillan, 1990.

[7]Author interview.

BRIGHT IDEAS

Sometimes it helps to be a little mad. Most great ideas have been laughed at. And, truth to tell, sometimes inventors become a little carried away at the possibilities: Jacob Schick, inventor of the electric razor, believed that by shaving correctly every day, a man could live to be 120 years old. He was wrong, but he was right about the market potential for an electric razor.

The second truism associated with bright business ideas is that you make your own luck. In 1979 a Hewlett-Packard engineer found that when metal was heated in a specific way, it splattered all over. The decision to exploit this feature launched the ink-jet printer business. Ten years later, this decision became the basis for over $6 billion in H-P revenues.

Consider the rise of the Mark McCormack business empire. This can be traced back to the decision by Arnold Palmer to allow golf enthusiast and lawyer McCormack to organize a few exhibitions for him. Palmer's lucrative rise to legendary status was ignited by McCormack, whose International Management Group (founded in 1962) created the business of sports.

Look at the story of the creation of the credit card. In 1950 Frank McNamara found himself in a restaurant with no money and came up with the idea of the Diners Club Card. The credit card changed the acts of buying and selling throughout the world.

Conclusion? Luck may come your way, but *you* still have to convert it into business reality.

Great Decision #60

Innovation and bright ideas take time to develop. While on vacation in 1943, Edwin Land decided to go for a walk to contemplate a problem posed by his daughter. As Land walked he invented the Polaroid camera.

In the 1930s a young woman named Helen Maislen was a physics student at Smith College in Boston. She met another physics student from Norwich College, Edwin Land, and they married. Land later went to Harvard, and became obsessed with the phenomenon of polarization.

In 1937, Land established a company that made a polarizing plastic. He gave it the name Polaroid; his wife's professor had actually used the term first. The business took off. Then, in 1943, Land found himself with his family in Santa Fe, enjoying a vacation. He took photographs of his family, like any doting father. His three-year-old daughter bemoaned the fact that they had to wait so long to see the photographs developed.

The idea of combining the polarization technology with developing films struck a chord in Land's fertile imagination. There was something to it. He decided to take a walk. Along the way, as he padded the streets of Santa Fe, Land developed the concept for the Polaroid camera.

Turning it into reality proved a little harder. By 1950, Land had a system that produced black-and-white images. It took until 1959 for him to develop a color version, which reached the market in 1963.

The Polaroid camera took off. By the late 1960s, it was calculated that half of American households owned a Polaroid camera of some sort.

THE GREATEST LESSONS

Call a time-out.   Calling a time-out is not restricted to sports arenas. Businesspeople could learn a few lessons. When the heat is on, a time-out can work wonders. Take a walk. Sip on a coffee. Stare into the distance. Land knew the value of thinking and gave himself the space to think.

Obsess.   Land decided that there was a solution and he worked until he found it. "Anything worth doing is worth doing to excess," he said—and he did. Altogether he amassed more than 530 patents.

Great Decision #61

Ray Kroc liked Mac and Dick McDonald's stand in San Bernardino, California that sold hamburgers, fries, and milkshakes—so much so that he decided to buy the rights and then franchise them, creating a huge global company and a vast market for fast food.

The two McDonald brothers, Dick and Maurice (known by all as Mac), opened up a restaurant in San Bernardino, California in 1940. It was nothing unusual—a barbecue and carhop place. As they became more experienced, the McDonald's realized that their customers wanted food in a hurry. They didn't want to be waited on, necessarily. They just wanted their food quickly. So in December 1948, Dick and Mac moved into fast food. Their new restaurant was topped by a large neon sign proclaiming that Speedee the Chef worked there.

It wasn't a particularly sophisticated sort of place. Dick came up with the idea of a couple of arches to represent the letter *M* and put tiles (red and white) on the walls so that they could be cleaned easily. Customers could drive in and place their orders at the first window. There weren't many choices, but by the time they'd driven to the next window, their order was ready. The customers loved it. It was cheap and easy; a hamburger cost 15 cents, a malt drink 20 cents, and a pack of fries 10 cents.

The customers flocked in and the McDonald brothers expanded their empire. Eventually they had eight restaurants, all following the same formula. (Only one still stands, in east Los Angeles.) Their success came to the attention of Ray Kroc (1902–1984), a kitchen equipment salesman who sold marketing rights to milkshake mixers. "I've never waited in line for a hamburger in my whole life," said Kroc when he visited the McDonald's restaurant. "Some way I've got to become involved in this."

In 1954 Kroc bought the American franchise for McDonald's for $2.7 million, and in 1961 he bought the world rights. The rest is history. As the McDonald brothers stepped back into branding mythology, Kroc took over the world.

"It is hard to believe McDonald's was once a locally owned single-site facility when now it can be found anywhere in the world," says Ann

Marucheck of the University of North Carolina's Kenan-Flagler Business School.

Kroc brought dynamism to the chain, combined with his own distinct business philosophy: "Persistence and determination alone are omnipotent." "If a corporation has two executives who think alike, one is unnecessary." Here is Kroc on helping your neighbor: "If I saw a competitor drowning I'd put a live fire hose in his mouth." The 100th McDonald's opened in 1959; the first outside the United States in 1967; and, in 1990, the last bastion fell when McDonald's opened in Moscow. Russians couldn't buy anything in their supermarkets, but could admire the efficiency of capitalism at work as the entire foreign community in Moscow ate at McDonald's.

The ninth restaurant in the McDonald's chain, and Kroc's first, was in Des Plaines, Illinois. McDonald's headquarters is located nearby at Oak Brook. Today, McDonald's has 24,500 restaurants in 114 countries around the world. A staggering 38 million people eat at a McDonald's restaurant every single day of the week.

The formula is astonishingly universal (international sales account for 60 percent of McDonald's earnings): limited choice, quick service, and clean restaurants. While McDonald's is successful around the world, there is nothing particularly original or innovative about what it does. You don't have to be one of the Le Roux brothers to serve up a tasty cheeseburger. Instead, McDonald's does the simple things well. A McDonald's restaurant in Nairobi, Kenya looks much the same as one in Warsaw, Poland or Battle Creek, Michigan. (Even so, some allowances are made for local tastes, such as lamb burgers in India and kosher burgers in Israel.) It is, McDonald's proclaims, the "most successful food service organization in the world."

McDonald's still possesses the all-conquering self-esteem of a global powerhouse. Its publicity material notes with some regret that, "On any day, even as the market leader, McDonald's serves less than one percent of the world's population."

THE GREATEST LESSONS

Insist on consistent quality.   Henry Ford mastered mass production of products; McDonald's has mastered mass production of service. It has done so through strict adherence to simple beliefs. Quality, cleanliness, and uniformity form the basis of the McDonald's brand. Kroc was obsessive about these issues. "It requires a certain kind of mind to see beauty in a hamburger bun," he reflected. He was right; no one else manages to do the simple things as well. In effect, the very uniformity of the brand is the crucial differentiating factor.

Maintain control.   Kroc created a culture based on control rather than creativity. Franchise holders were not expected to think of things by themselves. They were told what to deliver. In many ways the problems now faced by McDonald's were tackled by many other brands some years ago. McDonald's, for example, is heavily centralized. Its cadre of middle and senior managers tends to have come up through the ranks. Different voices have been notable in their absence. It has also generally ignored segmenting its markets. "The old model of just telling people what to do was exactly the right model for a long, long time," says current CEO, Jack Greenberg. "Now we need a different approach to managing that pays more attention to different market segments."

The other vital missing ingredient is innovation. McDonald's has proved an unimaginative and generally unsuccessful innovator. "We have been taking much too long to develop an idea and get it to the market, then too long to decide whether we want to do it or not," admits Greenberg. While Greenberg accepts that it must change, whether such a huge organization with such a strong culture can do so remains open to question.

See the opportunity.   Kroc's genius was in seeing the opportunity, in deciding to seize it, and then in deciding to franchise the concept around the world. After all, the McDonald brothers had the concept, but had taken it nowhere.

Great Decision #62

The decision made in China before 1000 BC proved significant. Without it, there would never have been Adam Smith or Gordon Ghekko. The decision was to manage buying and selling by using a cowrie shell as currency. It was bigger than a dollar and equally important.

Bright ideas come in a myriad of forms.

In 1930 Messrs. Eugene Ltd. of Dover Street, London decided to use closed-circuit television to advertise their permanent waving technique at the Hairdressing Fair of Fashion. The TV ad was born.

Around 59 BC Julius Caesar kept people up to date by issuing handwritten sheets that were distributed in Rome, as well as, it is suspected, using posters around the city. The greatness of leaders ever since has been partly measured by their ability to communicate.

Often the most powerful ideas involve attempts to systematize something that has previously been a mystery. In modern times, we can point to Pierre Du Pont's decision to implement financial management at Du Pont. During his time with the company (1902–1940), he developed modern corporate accounting, including concepts such as double-entry accounting, financial forecasting, and return on capital invested.

Looking deep into history, there were also major decisions that provided systems of measurement, means of understanding and means of trading. The Chinese Qin Dynasty (221–206 BC) produced the Great Wall, a fantastic management feat as well as an engineering coup. They also developed what is reputed to be the first reliable system of weights and measures. By deciding to develop a standard system, the Qins aided commercial development and set a helpful precedent.

Even further back, a decision made in China before 1000 BC proved significant. Without it, there would never have been Adam Smith or Gordon Ghekko. The decision was to manage buying and selling by using a cowrie shell as currency. It was bigger than a dollar and equally important. "Before coins were invented in China, cowrie shells were used as money," writes Joe Cribb.[1] "Payments of cowries as rewards are described in inscriptions on ancient Chinese bronzes of the second millennium BC. Chinese archeologists excavating tomb sites of the Shang period (sixteenth to eleventh centuries BC) have dug up large numbers of money cowries, often tied together in strings."

Other things that have been used as money, according to Glyn Davies, include amber, beads, drums, eggs, feathers, gongs, hoes, ivory, jade, leather, mats, nails, oxen, pigs, quartz, rice, salt, vodka, yarns, and salt.[2]

It is a daunting thought that cowrie shells were still used as currency in Nigeria within living memory.

THE GREATEST LESSONS

The desire for measurement is universal. People thrive on systems and on the to and fro of barter and trade. No one form of money developed. Instead, a myriad of different forms of currency emerged in different places throughout the world. Humans need money in a practical and spiritual sense, as well as a financial one.

Great Decision #63

In 1892, William Wrigley decided to offer two packs of chewing gum with each can of baking powder sold in his fledgling business. It worked so well that he decided to change his business to selling chewing gum.

In 1891, William Wrigley moved from Philadelphia to Chicago, where the company's headquarters are located today in the Wrigley Building at 410 North Michigan Avenue. He was twenty-nine years old and had just $32 to his name. His pockets may have been empty but his head was full of dreams. A natural salesman, Wrigley dreamed of starting his own business.

In Chicago he set up a business selling soap to the wholesale trade. Ahead of his time, Wrigley understood the benefits of free promotions. To make his products more attractive to buyers he offered gifts, including free baking powder. The baking powder proved more popular than the soap, so like any good entrepreneur, Wrigley moved out of the soap business and into the baking powder business.

And so it might have continued, had it not been for another of Wrigley's free promotions. In 1892, he decided to offer two packs of chewing gum with each can of baking powder sold. It was an even bigger hit than the free baking powder had been. Once again, Wrigley switched businesses. Chewing gum, he thought, was his future. This time he was right.

The first Wrigley chewing gums, Lotta Gum and Vassar, were launched that same year. They were followed in 1893 by Juicy Fruit and Wrigley's Spearmint. Those two flavors have been with us ever since.

By 1911, Wrigley's Spearmint was America's number one chewing gum and Wrigley was ready to spread his wings. He introduced PK chewing gum, which was sold in a tightly packed pellet form rather than loose in a box . The name, evidently, was inspired by the advertising slogan that accompanied it: "Packed Tight—Kept Right."

The company became a public corporation in 1919. Its stock was first listed on the New York Stock Exchange and the Midwest Stock Exchange in 1923. In 1944, Wrigley's entire production was turned over to the U.S. Armed Forces overseas and at sea (as was the production of Hershey chocolate). It may not have the same appeal today, but the slogan, "Got any gum, chum?" was a big hit with military personnel at the time.

After the Second World War, the invention of the teenager gave Wrigley's another huge boost. When they weren't puffing on cigarettes, rock 'n' roll rebels chewed gum. Its popularity was guaranteed by parents, who despised the constant jaw motion of their surly offspring and branded chewing gum a disgusting habit. This simply made Wrigley's product more popular than ever with the high school crowd.

As the century advanced and American consumers became ever more hygiene conscious, fresh breath became a serious issue. Once again, Wrigley's rode to the rescue. Chewing gum had the additional benefit of hiding the smell of cigarettes and alcohol—or so millions of teenagers and errant spouses believed.

The years were kind to Wrigley's. It had the good fortune to be in business at a time when American culture was being exported all over the world. The process was started by the archetypal gum-chewing GI in World War II, and was immortalized by Hollywood. The demand for all things American meant that domestic chewing gums, like domestic cigarettes, were just no substitute for the genuine article. The mass marketing of America was and is a triumph of branding.

The irony is that many American-branded products are no longer made in America. Today, Wrigley's produces its distinctively packaged chewing gum in 13 factories around the world. It is unlikely to go back to selling soap.

THE GREATEST LESSONS

Be flexible enough to change.   Today's successful product range is tomorrow's failure. If you see an opportunity, follow it.

Advertise.   Wrigley's natural gift for marketing played an important role in the development of the business. He was one of the first entrepreneurs to appreciate the power of branding. To begin with, he concentrated his efforts on his Spearmint gum, advertising it in newspapers. By 1907 he was ready to expand his advertising efforts, but his plans coincided with an economic downturn that hit the Chicago business community. While other companies cut back on their advertising, Wrigley did the opposite. He saw this as the ideal time to get extra attention for his business by advertising. He stepped up his branding efforts and increased production.

Look abroad.   By the time World War I started, Wrigley's was expanding overseas. In 1915, the company established its first factory in Australia, and by 1927, the famous gum went into production in the U.K. World War II gave the business a boost as the allied armed forces purchased large quantities of chewing gum, which was believed to ease tension, promote alertness, and improve morale generally.

Great Decision #64

The decision of the Wilsons of Memphis to go on a motoring vacation was initially unsuccessful. It was not a great deal of fun staying in expensive and poor-quality motels. So Kemmons Wilson decided to build his own. The first Holiday Inn was opened in Memphis in 1952.

In the summer of 1951, the Wilson family of Memphis set off on a motoring vacation. There was nothing special about it, just a married couple and their five children heading to Washington, D.C. Kemmons Wilson was a Memphis builder and realtor. He and his family became exasperated as their vacation progressed. It was not a great deal of fun staying in expensive and poor-quality motels.

"A motel room only cost about $8 a night, but the proprietors inevitably charged $2 extra for each child. So the $8 charge soon ballooned into an $18 charge for my family," Wilson later recounted. "If we could get a room with two beds, our two daughters slept in one, and Dorothy and I slept in the other. Our three boys slept on the floor in sleeping bags. Sometimes there was a dollar deposit for the key and another dollar for the use of a television."

So Wilson (born in 1913) decided to build his own motel. "I was seized by an idea: I could build a chain of affordable hotels, stretching from coast to coast. Families could travel cross-country and stay at one of my hotels every night." Wilson envisaged 400 such motels. It sounded outrageously ambitious, but Wilson didn't hesitate. He began work while still on vacation. He measured rooms and looked at facilities. His conclusion was that features such as televisions, telephones, ice machines, and restaurants should be universal. In his imagined hotel chain, children would stay free.

When the family returned home, Wilson got straight to work. He asked a draftsman to draw up some plans. The draftsman had seen a Bing Crosby film the previous evening and labeled the plan Holiday Inn, after the Crosby movie. Wilson liked it, and the name stuck.

The first Holiday Inn was opened in Memphis in 1952. (It fared better than Wilson's first house, which he mistakenly built on the wrong lot.) The rest is motel history. Clean and cheap, Holiday Inns sprouted up throughout the United States and then the world. "He changed the way American travels," Senator John Glenn concluded of Wilson.

"Kemmons Wilson has transformed the motel from the old wayside fleabag into the most popular home away from home," noted *Time*. By the time Wilson retired in 1979, Holiday Inn was the world's largest lodging chain. Today there are 1,643 Holiday Inn hotels with 327,059 rooms.

After coming up with the idea and launching the first Holiday Inn at 4985 Summer Avenue, Kemmons Wilson attempted to franchise the idea. Opening four Holiday Inns in just over a year in Memphis had stretched his finances to their limits. Twelve franchises were sold to housebuilders for $500 each. Only three were eventually built. Wilson thought again and sold 120,000 shares in the company at $9.75 each. This provided the capital necessary to create a nationwide chain. The fiftieth Holiday Inn was opened in 1958; the one-hundredth in 1959; and the five-hundredth in 1964.

In 1979, Wilson gave control of Holiday Inns to his two sons. Since then, Holiday Inn has been controlled by a number of corporate names. Holiday Inn is now part of the large U.K.-based leisure and entertainment group Bass, which is owner or franchiser of over 2,600 Intercontinental, Crowne Plaza, Holiday Inn, Holiday Inn Express, and Staybridge Suites. Holiday Inn remains the most widely recognized lodging brand in the world. Bass is now building what it labels the "Holiday Inn of the Future." Kemmons Wilson is watching.

THE GREATEST LESSONS

Follow the idea through.   We've all had bright ideas, but usually they lie dormant. Kemmons Wilson turned his bright idea into reality.

Use both luck and brains.   Wilson attributes his success to a combination of timing and sound business thinking; his autobiography is entitled *Half Luck, Half Brains*. Away from Holiday Inn, Kemmons Wilson has continued in his entrepreneurial way. In his late sixties, he put his fortune on the line to build Orange Lack Country Club in Kissimmee, Florida. It became the world's largest timeshare resort, with nearly 60,000 owners. Kemmons Wilson's companies ("Over fifty businesses ranging from pork rinds to candy," Wilson has said) now include Wilson Air Center, Wilson Hotel Management Company, Wilson-Todd Construction, and Wilson Graphics.

Great Decision #65

In the 1970s Gillette was under threat from all sides. Competition was pushing it downmarket. It cut prices and profits plummeted. Predators waited. Then it made a decision that turned the company around: Its place was at the high-quality, premium-price end of the market. Period.

Sometimes companies forget what they are good at. They become distracted, take their eyes off the ball, and usually watch helplessly as profits plummet.

That is exactly what was happening to Gillette in the 1970s. As cheap throwaway razors made their presence felt in its markets, it was pushed relentlessly downmarket. "The critics didn't understand the real problem. It was that Gillette had lost sight of what its brand was," observed Bradley Gale of the Strategic Planning Institute. "Marketers can create brand power and superior returns almost anywhere—if they focus on becoming perceived quality leaders."[3]

Then Gillette realized that quality mattered and that innovation rather than relentless price cutting was the soul of its business. Its great decision, therefore, was to invest in the development of the Sensor range of razor blades. It decided to take its foot off the price-cutting pedal and take time to develop a genuine market-changing product.

This process actually began in 1979, but the Sensor wasn't introduced until 1990. Gillette spent $275 million on designing and developing the range. Sensor has been one of the great business successes of recent years. By 1995 it accounted for $2.6 billion in sales. With 68 percent of the U.S. wet shaving market and 73 percent of the European market, competitors haven't made any inroads into Sensor's domination.

Since then Gillette has carved out a lucrative niche for itself in what is labeled male and female grooming as well as in a number of areas, including alkaline batteries. Gillette's empire now includes Braun electrical appliances; toiletries and cosmetics; stationery products (it owns Parker and Papermate pens); Oral-B toothbrushes; and the battery maker Duracell, with which Gillette merged in 1996. Little wonder that it is estimated that over 1.2 billion people use a Gillette product every day. This explains why the company had 1997 sales of $10.1 billion and has 44,000 employees working in 63 facilities in 26 countries.

Gillette's fans include Warren Buffett, who has commented: "I go to bed happy at night, knowing that hair is growing on billions of male faces." For investors like Buffett, Gillette has a number of attractions. Most notably, Gillette appears to have struck a balance between innovation and the marketplace. "Good products come out of market research," says CEO Alfred Zeien. "Great products come from R&D. And blockbusters are born when something great comes out of the lab at the same time people want it." Zeien, like Warren Buffett and company founder King Gillette, takes the long view. He points to similarities between Gillette developing new products and the long-term R&D necessary to develop new drugs.

THE GREATEST LESSONS

Don't get caught doing what the competition is doing.   With stores filling with Bics and other disposable brands, Gillette made the mistake of competing at the same level. It basically sought to out-Bic Bic. It couldn't. Aping the competition is not a strategy; it's a cop-out.

Think and act globally.   Gillette is truly global in its reach and operations. Over 70 percent of its sales and profits come from outside the United States. No less an authority than Rosabeth Moss Kanter has said, "Gillette does internationally what every company should be doing." Gillette can only hope that it continues to be so little emulated.

Bright ideas take time.   "Invent something people use and throw away," a wise person told King Camp Gillette (1855–1932) in 1895. Gillette started thinking. Later he thought of a disposable safety razor. Then he met the inventor William Nickerson. The Gillette company started its life in 1901 on the Boston waterfront as the Gillette Safety Razor Company, with Gillette trying to persuade investors to put their money into a company with an untested product. (The name Nickerson wasn't featured, because it suggested nicking yourself while shaving.) It was not until 1903 that the company began production of its razor sets and blades.

During its first year, Gillette sold 51 razor sets and 168 blades. By 1905 it was selling 250,000 razor sets and nearly 100,000 blade packages, and by 1915, sales had increased to the point that the company was selling 7 million blades a year. In 1917 the U.S. government placed an order for 3.5 million razors and 36 million blades. The entire army needed a shave. In 1923, Gillette produced a gold-plated razor, a snip at a dollar. (By this time, King Gillette had disappeared into the sunset of Los Angeles to convert his experience into social theories.)

Great Decision #66

In 1970, Spencer Sylver of 3M invented the Post-It Note. But it took Arthur Fry to recognize the opportunity in 1979. The Post-It remains a ubiquitous money-spinner.

Innovation often involves putting two and two together and making four. A simple idea from one place combined with a simple idea from another place can yield gold. That's the story of Art Fry and the Post-It.

Fry started working for 3M in 1953 when he was still a chemical engineering student at the University of Minnesota. His career was spent in developing new products for his highly innovative employer.

The Post-It was invented when Fry's colleague, Dr. Spencer Silver in 3M's Central Research Department, came up with a weak adhesive that stuck strongly enough to keep pieces of paper together that could then be separated without leaving a mark. It was an invention in search of a use.

Fry came up with the use. As a chorister in his church choir, he used pieces of paper to mark pages. These had a habit of falling out. "I needed a bookmark that would stay put, yet could easily be removed without damaging my hymnal," said Fry. Then, eureka! Fry used the adhesive to stick pieces of paper into his book as bookmarks. "Now I had a bookmark that could stick to the page while exposing a part that wasn't sticky," he said. Fry then used the bookmark and adhesive to mark a report. "That's when I came to the very exciting realization that my sticky bookmark was actually a new way to communicate and organize information."

Of course, great ideas routinely fail in the marketplace. The Post-It, as it was called, was no exception. In 1977 it was tested in Richmond, Tulsa, Denver, and Tampa. Consumers were notable by their absence; after all, no one really knew what the product could be used for.

Inspiration came when two 3M executives flew to Richmond and walked into offices to demonstrate the product. Once they knew how it could be used and the myriad of possibilities, people bought Post-Its on the spot. Of the people who saw the Post-It at work, 90 percent said they'd buy.

The pilot was expanded to 11 sites. Before long Post-Its were everywhere. Art Fry advertised Gap clothing as a result; George Jones mentioned the product in a song; books by Dick Francis and Tom Clancy featured them; and the product even had walk-on "parts" in *Seinfeld*.

THE GREATEST LESSONS

2+2 = 4.   But only if you work in a culture that encourages connections to be made between different people and different ideas.

Selling is about human interaction.   The groundswell behind Post-Its began when two execs got on a plane and started visiting offices to show them to people. Without their intervention, Post-Its could well have flopped.

Invest in innovation.   The Post-It took a long time to develop a following. It was a germ of an idea. It took 3M's backing to make it happen. R&D takes investment and an appetite for risk taking. (Perhaps the ultimate R&D decision was the one by Queen Isabella of Spain, to sponsor Columbus' voyage to the New World.)

Notes

[1]Cribb, Joe, *Money: From Cowrie Shells to Credit Cards,* Knopf, 1990.

[2]Davies, Glyn, *A History of Money,* University of Wales Press, 1996.

[3]Peters, Tom, *Liberation Management,* Knopf, 1992.

PEOPLE POWER

People have had a bad time at the hands of managers through the ages. The humble employee has been commonly regarded as a robotic automaton. Describing his theory of Scientific Management, Frederick Taylor said: "Brutally speaking, our scheme does not ask any initiative in a man. We do not care for his initiative." Employees had to be told the optimum way to do a job and then they had to do it. "Each employee should receive every day clear-cut, definite instructions as to just what he is to do and how he is to do it, and these instructions should be exactly carried out, whether they are right or wrong," Taylor advised. Not surprisingly this did not always go over well. In 1911 the introduction of Taylor's methods caused a strike at a munitions factory run by the Army.

A reminder of the basic humanity of good management comes from Peter Drucker. "Management is tasks. Management is discipline. But management is also people," he says. "Every achievement of management is the achievement of a manager. Every failure is the failure of a manager. People manage, rather than *forces* or *facts*. The vision, dedication and integrity of managers determine whether there is management or mismanagement." Management is personal. Management is fundamentally concerned with maximizing the potential and performance of people.

Inevitably, some are better at it than others. How many CEOs have you heard pronounce that people are the company's most important assets? Plenty. How many mean it? How many actually convert that trite corporate truism into practice, day in and day out? Not many. "By the time people become CEOs they are preoccupied with survival and money. They respond to capital markets, stockholders, and so on. Even if they try or want to be people-oriented, a financial crisis will always get their attention first," says MIT's Ed Schein.

Great Decision #67

In 1914 Henry Ford decided to pay his workers $5 a day. It was a great leap forward for human resource management, but it was not a benevolent decision. Ford effectively created the market for his own product.

In terms of management, Ford was an atheist with attitude. In the same way that Ford didn't believe in Models Ts in different colors with fins and extras, he didn't believe in management. "Fundamental to Henry Ford's misrule was a systematic, deliberate and conscious attempt to run the billion-dollar business without managers. The secret police that spied on all Ford executives served to inform Henry Ford of any attempt on the part of one of his executives to make a decision," noted Peter Drucker in *The Practice of Management.*[1]

As a result, production in the Ford company's huge plant was based on strict functional divides—demarcations. Ford believed in people getting on with their jobs and not raising their heads above functional parapets. He didn't want engineers talking to salespeople, or any people making decisions without his say-so.

The methods used by Ford were grim and unforgiving. "How come when I want a pair of hands I get a human being as well?" he complained. In his book, *My Life and Work,* Ford offered a chilling insight into the new industrial logic. He calculated that the production of a Model T required 7,882 different operations. Of these 949 required "strong, able-bodied, and practically physical perfect men" and 3,338 required "ordinary physical strength." The remainder, said Ford, could be undertaken by "women or older children" and "670 could be filled by legless men, 2,637 by one-legged men, two by armless men, 715 by one-armed men and 10 by blind men."

Not surprisingly, Ford will never be celebrated for his humanity or his people-management skills. Among his many innovations was a single human one: Ford introduced the $5 wage for his workers, at the time about twice the average for the industry. Skeptics suggest that the only reason he did this was so that his workers could buy Model Ts of their own.

Ford's decision to increase wages was a direct response to the sheer tedium of working on one of his production lines. His staff turnover was increasing rapidly. In response, Ford upped wages from $2.50 to $5 a day. At the same time he made the working day eight hours instead of nine.

GREATEST LESSONS

Retain your staff.   Henry Ford may not have been the most humanitarian employer in the world, but he realized the importance of retaining staff. If he had invested in their training, it was worth doubling their wages to ensure they didn't go anywhere else.

Employees are human too.   There is little evidence that Henry Ford ever really recognized the humanity of those he employed. If he had, he would have been a better man and, who knows, his company might have been even more successful.

Great Decision #68

Among 3M's many innovations was the decision to allow any of its researchers to dedicate 15 percent of their time to their own projects. Freedom and creativity ensued and were ensured.

"Don't follow everybody else. Get off the beaten track. Be a little mad," advises Jean Paulucci. Give people time and you don't know what will emerge. 3M did just that with its 15 percent policy. What freedom from the corporate yoke! The 15 percent policy is called, among other things, "the bootleg policy." It could also be called a competitive advantage, because it has helped foster and nurture so many good ideas (most notably the Post-It).

The 15 percent policy encourages researchers to roam further afield. Hajime Mitari, the president of Canon, has said, "We should do something when people say it is crazy. If people say something is good, it means that someone else is already doing it." Much the same thinking applies at 3M.

"The object is to spur as many ideas as possible, because perhaps one in a thousand will turn out to fit," explains Post-It developer Art Fry. "An idea might be a perfectly good idea for another company, but not for yours. Putting together a new product is like putting together a jigsaw puzzle made of raw material suppliers, distributors, government regulations, the amount of capital you have to spend. If one part doesn't fit, the whole project can fail. Your work might have been brilliant but somebody else dropping the ball can lead to failure."

THE GREATEST LESSONS

Time and space help creativity. Freed from the day-to-day pressures of deadlines, smart and brilliant ideas can emerge. If you don't give people time and space, you may be cutting out a hefty proportion of their best ideas.

Don't be scared of failure. Innovation has to be fearless. Any company that is scared to fail will fail to meet 3M's standards of innovation.

Innovation creates competitive advantage. "Pioneering don't pay," said Andrew Carnegie. He was wrong. It pays so long as it is managed imaginatively.

Great Decision #69

In the years immediately after World War II, the young Hewlett-Packard company was struggling. Its wartime sources of work had dried up. Its decisive response? It decided to hire some of the talented people available for work after the war and their talents helped it innovate itself into the future.

"You shouldn't gloat about anything you've done; you ought to keep going and try to find something better to do," said David Packard (1912–1996), cofounder of the company that still bears his name. Hewlett-Packard (H-P) is akin to IBM in the 1960s: everyone's epitome of a well-managed company. It is associated with excellence. Indeed, when they were assembling their list of excellent companies in the late 1970s, Tom Peters and Robert Waterman included Hewlett-Packard. It was one of their least controversial choices. Similarly, when Jerry Porras and James Collins wrote *Built to Last,* their celebration of long-lived companies, there was no doubt that Hewlett-Packard was worthy of inclusion. In 1985, *Fortune* ranked Hewlett-Packard as one of the two most highly admired companies in America. The company is ranked similarly in virtually every other poll on well-managed companies or ones that would be good to work for. H-P has pulled off an unusual double: It is both admired and successful.

Hewlett-Packard began in 1937 when, with a mere $538 and a rented garage in Palo Alto, Bill Hewlett and Dave Packard set up a business. The two had met while students at nearby Stanford. Their ambitions were typical of many young people starting a business. "We thought we would have a job for ourselves. That's all we thought about in the beginning," said Packard. "We hadn't the slightest idea of building a big company." The garage was the birthplace of Silicon Valley.

In their first year of business Hewlett and Packard achieved sales of $5,100, with $1,300 in profits. Hewlett-Packard's first success was a device for measuring sound waves that they sold to Walt Disney. An automatic lettuce thinner and a shock machine to help people lose weight followed. They also pondered the market opportunities for automatic urinal flushers, bowling alley sensors, and air conditioning equipment. The duo left the garage for good in 1940.

During wartime the business flourished, employing 144 people at its height. Immediately after the war, sales fell off, by half in 1946 alone.

Undaunted, Hewlett and Packard hired technical talent, which was then plentiful as industries adapted to postwar life. The decision to take the risk of hiring people on the off chance that their talent would enable the company to turn the corner paid off. The business revived. By 1948, the company's sales were $2.1 million.

Their secret, said Hewlett and Packard, lay in the simplicity of their methods. "Professors of management are devastated when I say we were successful because we had no plans. We just took on odd jobs," said Hewlett. But their legacy is not the efficiency of their lettuce thinner or the quality of their urinal flusher; it is the culture of the company they created and the management style they used to run it, the H-P way.

From the very start, Hewlett-Packard followed a few fundamental principles. It did not believe in long-term borrowing to secure the expansion of the business. Its recipe for growth was simply that its products needed to be leaders in their markets. It got on with the job. "Our main task is to design, develop, and manufacture the finest [electronic equipment] for the advancement of science and the welfare of humanity. We intend to devote ourselves to that task," said Packard in a 1961 memo to employees.

The duo eschewed fashionable management theory. "If I hear anybody talking about how big their share of the market is or what they're trying to do to increase their share of the market, I'm going to personally see that a black mark gets put in their personnel folder," Packard said in a 1974 speech.

The company believed that people could be trusted and should always be treated with respect and dignity. "We both felt fundamentally that people want to do a good job. They just need guidelines on how to do it," said Packard.

H-P believed that management should be available and involved; Management by Wandering Around was the motto. Indeed, rather than the administrative suggestions of management, Packard preferred to talk of leadership. If there was conflict, it had to be tackled through communication and consensus rather than confrontation. "Their legacy, and the achievement that Packard was most proud of, is a management style based on openness and respect for the individual," noted Louise Kehoe of the *Financial Times* in Packard's obituary. Former CEO John Young has observed: "Our basic principles have endured intact since our founders conceived them. We distinguish between core values, and practices; the core values don't change, but the practices might."

Hewlett-Packard was a company built on very simple ideas. While all about were turning into conglomerates, Hewlett and Packard kept their heads down and continued with their methods. When their divisions grew too big—and by that they meant around 1,500 people—they split them up to ensure that they didn't spiral out of control.

They kept it simple. Nice guys built a nice company. They didn't do anything too risky or too outlandish. (Packard was skeptical about pocket calculators though, in the end, the company was an early entrant into the market.) They didn't bet the company on a big deal or get into debt. Indeed, in his research Richard Pascale, author of *Managing on the Edge,* identified "terminal niceness" as a potential problem for the company. Being criticized for being too good could only happen in the business world. For living up to their simple standards, Hewlett-Packard deserves acknowledgement.

GREATEST LESSONS

Recruit talented people … no matter what.   Talented people will get you out of trouble. The problem comes when talented people won't work for you or you can't find them.

Trust people and they will repay that trust.   During the 1970s recession, Hewlett-Packard staff took a 10 percent pay cut and worked 10 percent fewer hours. If the company hadn't had a long-term commitment to employee stock ownership, perhaps employees wouldn't have been so keen to make sacrifices. The company also took advantage of lucky breaks that would have been missed elsewhere. In 1979 one of its engineers found that when metal was heated in a specific way, it splattered all over. The decision to exploit this technology launched the ink-jet printer business.

Great Decision #70

In the manner of a modern CEO, Emperor Hadrian (76–138) managed the vast Roman Empire by traveling addictively. Along the way he ordered that mines should all have bath houses so the miners could wash after work. This made him popular with miners, but not in Rome. Unfortunately, enlightened management of human resources remained the exception rather than the rule.

Little is known about Hadrian. The enigmatic wall builder was Roman Emperor from 117 to 138. What is known, or surmised, suggests that he was a champion of people power long before the advent of such niceties as human resource departments. Pomp and circumstance were not for him. Indeed, Hadrian's humane tendencies have led some historians to describe him as an "essentially modern personality" and a "modern monarch."

Hadrian joined the army as a young man. His reputation there was forged on his willingness to share the same conditions as his troops. One anecdote describes his refusal to wear his cloak or cap, no matter what the weather. Similarly, Hadrian was reputed to join his troops on lengthy marches in full armor.

A series of other humanitarian decisions cemented his reputation. He prohibited castration, and ordered humane treatment of slaves. Hadrian was also a globe-trotter. He didn't seek to control his empire from Rome, but traveled throughout it. In modern parlance, he accepted the diversity of his empire. Coins issued during his reign celebrated the numerous provinces he had visited. Hadrian also brought an end to the inexorable Roman expansionism. He sought to draw a line around the Empire rather than engage in endless foreign wars.

Hadrian was also reputed to have had an eye for financial management, though he started his reign by announcing an amnesty of all debts owed to the government. While his predecessor frittered away the money in the treasury, Hardian was more frugal and built up reserves to fund building projects and social welfare programs. At the same time, he was able to avoid raising taxes. (Modern politicians would no doubt like to know exactly how he managed to achieve the political equivalent of squaring the circle.)

THE GREATEST LESSONS

Leaders must be able to identify with the feelings, experiences, and fears of their followers.   Hadrian left headquarters and understood what it was like in the front line. He provided a more humane environment for soldiers and workers unused to being treated in such a way.

Being good doesn't necessarily make you more popular.   Hadrian is remembered for his wall building and little else. At the time, he was also little understood and not universally loved. Pity.

Great Decision #71

In 1956 GE established a center for executive development at Crotonville, New York. Its decision to invest in development has played a crucial role in the company's continuing success, and has inspired others to follow suit.

Ralph Cordiner, GE CEO in the 1950s, left an indelible mark on the company: In 1956 he created GE's now legendary Management Development Institute at Crotonville. The Institute established GE's determination to develop its people. Its tradition is carried on by today's CEO, Jack Welch. "I want a revolution, and I want it to start at Crotonville," Welch pronounced. Welch is a regular visitor and teacher at the center. It is estimated that in 250 sessions he has personally talked to some 15,000 of the company's executives.

The message of Crotonville is that developing people is too important a task to be delegated to business schools or training companies. Crotonville's director says that its mission "is to leverage GE's global competitiveness as an instrument of cultural change, by improving business acumen, leadership abilities, and organization effectiveness of GE professionals." Echoing Welch, Noel Tichy (now of the University of Michigan and an ex-Crotonville director) has called Crotonville "a staging ground for a corporate revolution."[2]

Putting such bold statements to one side, there is little doubt that Crotonville has given GE a clear head start over most of its rivals. Few other companies have managed to adapt the best managerial ideas to their particular circumstances with such frequency and over such an extended period of time. From Management by Objectives in the 1950s to Six Sigma in the 1990s, GE has effectively picked and chosen management ideas. Crotonville has also helped imbue generations of managers with the GE culture. (Such is its power that in his work on corporate culture, MIT's Ed Schein has made comparisons between the activities of Crotonville and similar institutions and wartime brainwashing. To some, this would be a compliment.)

Only now is the Crotonville model becoming fashionable. The trend toward do-it-yourself management development is strongest in the United States, where over 1,000 corporate colleges are now operating. They come in all shapes and sizes, and cover virtually every industry. The Ohio automotive parts manufacturer, Dana Corporation, has Dana

University; Ford has a Heavy Truck University in Detroit; Intel runs a university in Santa Clara; Sun Microsystems has Sun U; and Apple has its own university in Cupertino, California.

The growth in corporate universities can largely be attributed to two factors. First, critics of traditional business schools have accused them repeatedly of being too far from the pulse of the business world. It is a widely perceived weakness that corporate universities are keen to capitalize on. B-rated business schools can't get Jack Welch to deliver a lecture on leadership.

The second factor driving the growth of corporate universities is the realization that developing people is the key to future survival and too important to be delegated to an external organization. American researchers reported that companies with their own universities spent 2.5 percent of payroll on learning, double the U.S. national average. GE is not in the habit of delegating something that is important to an outside organization.

Clearly, with its teachers and resources, Crotonville is a huge investment. Corporate universities are not for the fainthearted. They are extremely expensive. Research in the United States by corporate university expert Jeanne Meister indicated that the average annual operating budget for a corporate university was $12.4 million (though 60 percent reported budgets of $5 million or less). Typically, National Semiconductor University, opened in 1994, occupies a 22,000 square foot premises with nine classrooms and room for 430 students. Such facilities, as business schools have been pointing out for years, are costly. Running Intel University cost that company $150 million in 1996. GE's Crotonville is an investment in people—a big investment.

THE GREATEST LESSONS

Develop people for the future.   Jack Welch not only connects with and develops people, but he also invests in the company's future. He is concerned about who will become the next CEO. He wants to exercise influence over the next cadre of management. He wants the GE way to exist long after his retirement. In many ways, Welch is passing on the baton. Reg Jones, his predecessor, did much the same, assiduously preparing Welch for his future role.

Training is leadership. Looking to the future and creating the next generation of executives is a central role of leadership. Leaving a power vacuum is hardly effective leadership. "Effective leaders recognize that the ultimate test of leadership is sustained success, which demands the constant cultivation of future leaders," says Noel Tichy.[3] Leaders must, therefore, invest in developing the leaders of tomorrow and they must communicate directly with those who will follow in their footsteps.

Leaders must teach. Noel Tichy believes that being able to pass on leadership skills to others requires three things. First, a leader must have a "teachable point of view": "You must be able to talk clearly and convincingly about who you are, why you exist, and how you operate."

Second, the leader requires a story. "Dramatic storytelling is the way people learn from one another," Tichy writes, suggesting that this explains why Bill Gates and the like feel the need to write books.

The third element in passing on the torch of leadership is teaching methodology. "To be a great teacher you have to be a great learner." The great corporate leaders are hungry to know more and do not regard their knowledge as static or comprehensive.

Welch passes all three tests with ease. He teaches at Crotonville and professes to enjoy it. He connects with people because he is keen to find out more about them and their problems.

Great Decision #72

What do you do on your first day after taking over the family business? The Brazilian Ricardo Semler fired 60 percent of the company's top management. Almost without thinking, he set in motion a revolution from which the rest of the business world is now anxious to learn.

Every week, groups of executives from leading multinationals visit a once unheard of company based in the outskirts of São Paulo, Brazil. The location is not the attraction; it's in a nondescript industrial complex. Nor is the company's technology exciting or its products, pumps and cooling units, the most thrilling in the world. The attraction lies in the revolutionary way the company is run.

When Ricardo Semler took over Semco from his father, he spent the first day firing 60 percent of the company's top management. Now Semco is a unique success story. It has managed to buck Brazilian commercial chaos, hyperinflation, and recession to increase productivity nearly sevenfold and profits fivefold.

Walking through the door, visiting executives immediately notice that there is no receptionist. Everyone at Semco is expected to meet his or her own visitors. There are no secretaries, nor are there any personal assistants. Managers do their own photocopying, send their own faxes, and make their own coffee. Semco has no dress code, so some people wear jackets and ties, others wear jeans.

But the Semco revolution goes far beyond this. "A few years ago, when we wanted to relocate a factory, we closed down for a day and everyone piled into buses to inspect three possible sites," recalls Ricardo Semler. "Their choice hardly thrilled the managers, since it was next to a company that was frequently on strike. But we moved in anyway."

Semco takes workplace democracy to previously unimagined frontiers. Everyone at the company has access to the books; managers set their own salaries; shopfloor workers set their own productivity targets and schedules; workers make decisions that were once the preserve of managers; even the distribution of the profit sharing scheme is determined by employees.

"We've taken a company that was moribund and made it thrive, chiefly by refusing to squander our greatest resource, our people," says Semler. Semler does not regard the transformation of Semco as a lesson to be emulated by other companies. Instead, he believes it simply points to the need for companies and organizations to reinvent themselves. "There *are* some companies that are prepared to change the way they work. They realize that nothing can be based on what used to be, that there is a better way. But 99 percent of companies are not ready, caught in an industrial Jurassic Park."

The plea for businesses to become more democratic and humane is a familiar one. The trouble, Semler candidly admits, is that listening to people, accepting their decisions, and inculcating people with the need for democracy is far from easy. "The era of using people as production tools is coming to an end," he argues. "Participation is infinitely more complex to practice than conventional unilateralism, but it is something that companies can no longer ignore or pay lip service to."

There is still a substantial amount of skepticism about Semco's approach and achievement, which Semler recorded in an international best-seller entitled *Maverick!* One eminent British executive commented after a public debate that Semler was "not a maverick; he's an eccentric."

It is little wonder that traditionalists among the management fraternity find Semler's message unpalatable. Managers are constantly appraised by Semco workers, rather than by a coterie of fellow executives, and they have to accept the idea that their decisions are not sacrosanct. Semler seems to be adept at biting his tongue when decisions don't go his way, and he admits, "There are a lot of people at Semco whose styles I don't actually like. I wouldn't have recruited them, but quite clearly they do their jobs effectively—otherwise people wouldn't support them."

Semler admits that it is too early to make cut-and-dried judgments about Semco's apparent revolution. "Really the work is only 30 percent completed," he estimates. "In the long term, success will come when the system forgets me and becomes self-perpetuating."

THE GREATEST LESSONS

Be true to your own beliefs.   Ricardo Semler could have continued managing the company in much the same way his father had done, but he was determined to shape it according to his own values.

Make yourself redundant.   As part of Semco's revolution, Semler has to a large extent become redundant. The chief executive's job rotates between five people. Diminished power is clearly not something that fills Semler with sadness; instead, it is confirmation that the Semco approach works. "I haven't hired or fired anyone for eight years or signed a company check. From an operational side I am no longer necessary, though I still draw a salary because there are many other ways of contributing to the company's success," he says. Indeed, Semler believes that what many consider the core activity of management—decision making—should not be management's function at all. "It's only when bosses give up decision-making and let their employees govern themselves that the possibility exists for a business jointly managed by workers and executives. That is true participative management."

Be your own role model.   The mistake people make, says Semler, is assuming that Semco is some kind of role model. "This is just one more version of how companies can organize themselves and succeed. Democracy alone will not solve all business problems. In fact, as we constantly see, nothing prevents autocratic companies from making money."

Great Decision #73

In 1981 Jan Carlzon, new chief of airline SAS, sent 10,000 front-line managers to two-day service seminars and sent 25,000 more managers to three-week courses. Within four months, SAS was the most punctual European airline and its service levels had been rejuvenated.

Jan Carlzon's work at Scandinavian Airlines in the 1980s is one of the most talked-about turnarounds of recent corporate history. SAS was an indifferent performer until Carlzon introduced it to customer service.

Most notably, Carlzon came up with the phrase "moments of truth"—the sequence of critical transactions across each stage of the ownership or use cycle.

These were broken down into:

- Initial contact
- First use
- Problem solving
- Ongoing support
- Further purchases
- Recommendations to others

Evaluating the degree to which satisfaction and value are affected at these different points in the cycle, and how they vary by customer type, can be the key to understanding customer behavior.

Carlzon proclaimed that "All business is show business," and he truly understood the process. Then he decided to prove the company's dedication to moments of truth by sending tens of thousands of SAS managers to training programs. It was a dramatic but meaningful decision. (There are parallels elsewhere. Larry Bossidy, CEO of AlliedSignal, put all the company's 86,000 employees through a development program and managed to speak to 15,000 of them during his first year on the job. Along the way, Bossidy also increased the market value of the company by 400 percent in six years.)

As a result of his decision, Carlzon set SAS on the road to revival and the company became a benchmark for international best practice in customer service. SAS has been celebrated by Tom Peters in *A Passion for Excellence,* among many others.

GREATEST LESSONS

Customer service is a management issue.   Too often, customer service is deemed to be the responsibility of front line operatives and no one else. Carlzon's decision to dispatch managers on customer service training programs got the message across forcefully that management was expected to understand and manage moments of truth with equal efficiency.

Communicate constantly.   Central to Carlzon's success was his dedication to communication. Jan Lapidoth worked with Carlzon at SAS in the 1980s and draws comparisons with another inveterate communicator, ABB's Percy Barnevik: "With Carlzon and Barnevik, there is a certain amount of showmanship. They play their roles to perfection. They stand in the middle of their strategy. They don't preach the strategy; they are the strategy. They communicate consistently and continually. They repeat the same messages again and again. It is like advertising, but they never grow tired of saying it—there is no sign of boredom, no cynicism, no sarcasm. They give words real meaning." This appetite for communication is clearly linked to a more humane style of management. The people deserve to be told.

Great Decision #74

Jack Welch succeeded Reg Jones in the top job at GE in 1981. This is one of the few instances of managerial succession being both planned and successful.

Jack Welch had a precocious climb up the General Electric hierarchy. In 1968, at the age of 33, he became GE's youngest general manager. Then he became senior vice president and sector executive for the consumer products and services sector, as well as vice chairman of the GE Credit Corporation. By 1979 he was vice chairman and executive officer. Along the way he built plastics into a formidable $2 billion business; turned around the medical diagnostics business; and began the development of GE Capital. His touch was sure.

The final leap to the uppermost reaches of the GE hierarchy came in 1977, when GE chairman Reg Jones suggested that Welch move to headquarters at Fairfield, Connecticut to join the race to succeed him. Jones knew what he was looking for in his successor. Pretty soon he recognized that Welch fitted the bill. "We need entrepreneurs who are willing to take well-considered business risks, and at the same time know how to work in harmony with a larger business entity," said Jones, a man honest enough to recognize his own limitations. "The intellectual requirements are light-years beyond the requirements of less complex organizations."

This is not to suggest that Jones' decision was made on the spot. Indeed, he began thinking about his successor in 1974 and came up with an initial shortlist of nearly 100 top-performing GE executives. This was reduced to six, who reported directly to the Corporate Executive Office. The six included Welch. "The management succession process that placed venerable General Electric in Welch's hands exemplifies the best and most vital aspects of the old GE culture," wrote Noel Tichy and Stratford Sherman. "Jones insisted on a long, laborious, exactingly thorough process that would carefully consider every eligible candidate, then rely on reason alone to select the best qualified. The result ranks among the finest examples of succession planning in corporate history."[4]

In December 1980, Welch was announced as the new CEO and chairman of GE. It was a record-breaking appointment. At 45, Welch was the youngest chief the company had ever appointed. Indeed, he was only the eighth CEO the company had appointed in 92 years.

Welch's dramatic tenure has elicited suggestions that Jones and his predecessors might not have approved of Welch's style. Far from it, other commentators respond. Jones knew exactly what he was doing. "When CEO Reginald Jones and the GE board of directors selected Jack Welch, they knowingly unleashed a prophet/crusader whose management perspective was a far cry from the analytical, administrative focus that dominated GE at that point in time," wrote Al Vicere and Robert Fulmer. "Welch brought a renewed sense of purpose to the company, one that helped GE regain its balance between the forces for innovative creativity and the forces for adaptive control."[5]

THE GREATEST LESSONS

Make succession planning a way of life.   At GE, one generation has handed the reins on to another seamlessly. All have been committed to change, to a greater or lesser extent. "GE's genius has been in its choice of successive CEOs, each of whom tended to counter the extremes of his predecessors," concluded Richard Pascale after studying the company's history.[6]

Indeed, their performance has been consistently good. In their book, Jerry Porras and Jim Collins report that Welch's record in his first decade in charge wasn't the best in GE's history. In fact, the celebrated CEO came in fifth place out of seven when measured by return on equity. "To have a Welch-caliber CEO is impressive. To have a century of Welch-caliber CEOs all grown from inside—well, that is one key reason why GE is a visionary company," conclude Porras and Collins.[7] It is a formidable record. No other large organization has been so successful in recruiting from within or has managed to sustain such consistent performance over such an extended period.

The roll call of GE CEOs is:

> *Charles Coffin:* Chairman and CEO from 1892 to 1922, Coffin was the leader of the group that bought Edison's patents and began the serious development of the business.
>
> *Gerard Swope:* Swope (1872–1957) joined GE in 1919 as the first president of International General Electric. He became president in

1922, with Owen Young as chairman. By the late 1920s the company had 75,000 employees and sales of $300 million. The company moved into the home appliances market. Swope emphasized the company's heritage as an engineering and manufacturing company and combined that with solid systems and, by the standards of the times, progressive human resource management. The Swope Plan of 1931 was one of the building blocks of the New Deal. Swope retired in 1939, but returned temporarily when his successor was appointed to wartime jobs.

Charles Wilson: Wilson's tenure, from 1940 until 1952, was interrupted by wartime work, a fact that made his impact and legacy less substantial than his predecessors.

Ralph Cordiner: Cordiner (1900–1973) was GE's CEO from 1950 until 1963. He was a robust champion of decentralization, which necessitated the creation of complex bureaucratic systems. His unsettling years in charge were notable for the introduction of Management by Objectives, a concept fashioned by a bright young management thinker named Peter Drucker who worked closely with the company at the time. Cordiner also launched GE Plastics and the company's aircraft engines business. He set up the company's Crotonville training center. Cordiner emphasized marketing and developed a new corporate slogan: "Progress is our most important product." His book, *New Frontiers for Professional Managers* (1956), summarized his managerial philosophy.

Fred Borch: Borch introduced GE to strategic planning and calmed things down a little from the Cordiner years. His impact is favorably recalled by Jack Welch: "Borch let a thousand flowers bloom. He got us into modular housing and entertainment businesses, nurtured GE Credit through its infancy, embarked on ventures in Europe, and let Aircraft Engine and Plastics alone so they could really get started. It became evident after he stepped down that General Electric had once again established a foothold into some businesses with a future."[8] Borch ruled the GE roost from 1964 until 1972.

Reg Jones: British-born Jones joined GE in 1939. In 1967 he became Chief Financial Officer, and was made CEO in 1973. Jones developed GE's business in high-tech markets such as jet engines and nuclear reactors, and sharpened up its financial systems. He was voted the most influential executive in the United States in 1979 and CEO of the Year in 1980. A former GE executive later commented: "During Jones' tenure, GE was financially strong but it was a dull, unexciting company. We were an organization in decline—and that was not recognized."[9] Jones' diligent succession planning led to Jack Welch, CEO.

Exercise commonsense management.   Another reason for GE's success is that it has been built around a simple, commonsense culture. Nothing fancy has distracted it. No thrills. Nothing too smart. "Sure we have good people, but we were all taken from the same pool as the people of all other companies, and yet I think we have something unique," ex-CEO Fred Borch said in 1965. "And our uniqueness, I think, is due to this matter of climate; respect for one another and working at our jobs to have as much darn fun out of it as we possibly can."

Great Decision #75

President McKinley's decision to appoint Elihu Root Secretary of War in 1899 took people by surprise. But, Root then successfully restructured the U.S. armed services—then in chaos—and instigated systems which ensured that the generals got back in touch with their people.

A friend of Theodore Roosevelt, the lawyer Elihu Root (1845–1937) was a renowned late nineteenth century dandy. Though well known in New York, where he was an active Republican, Root was all but unknown nationally when he was called up by McKinley to sort out the organizational chaos of the U.S. armed services.

The disorder among the fighting forces had been revealed in the Spanish-American War. A series of logistical disasters was symptomatic of a confused organization lacking in leadership. A post-war report lamented that the armed services were run in a manner ill befitting a corporation.

Root identified a lack of coordination among the various parts of the army as a key problem. He wanted to make the various army chiefs accountable and in touch. Too many, Root lamented, "had become entrenched in Washington armchairs." The Army's administration was reorganized; a War College established; and, among many other initiatives, a General Staff created.

Root's initiatives were later identified by Peter Drucker as "the first conscious and systematic application of management principles." At their heart was the simple matter of putting leaders and systems back in touch with people.

GREATEST LESSONS

Leaders need to be in constant touch with their people. Leaders are nothing without followers. Talented people are the engines of corporate and national success and renewal. Period.

Notes

[1]Drucker, Peter, *The Practice of Management*, Harper & Row, 1954.

[2]Tichy, Noel, and Sherman, Stratford, *Control Your Destiny or Someone Else Will*, Currency Doubleday, 1993.

[3]Tichy, Noel, "The mark of a winner," *Leader to Leader*, Fall 1997.

[4]Tichy, Noel, and Sherman, Stratford, *Control Your Own Destiny or Someone Else Will*, Currency Doubleday, 1993.

[5]Vicere, Albert, and Fulmer, Robert, *Leadership by Design*, Harvard Business School Press, 1998.

[6]Pascale, Richard, *Managing on the Edge*, Simon & Schuster, 1990.

[7]Porras, Jerry, and Collins, James, *Built to Last*, Century, 1997.

[8]Pascale, Richard, *Managing on the Edge*.

[9]Pascale.

THE HALL OF INFAMY

Perfection is impossible, especially in the business world where fear and failure lurk at every corner. Strangely, the worst decisions are inextricably linked to the greatest decisions. Somewhere there is always a loser. ("If you need any bad decisions, read the AT&T annual report. Any year will do," someone advised me acerbically.) There is always a flip side. But if you aren't prepared to fail, you won't succeed.

THE HALL OF INFAMY #1

In 1899, Asa Candler sold the bottling rights for Coca-Cola to Benjamin Thomas and Joseph Whitehead for $1. Candler thought the drink would be sold at soda fountains. He missed this trick, but few others.

THE HALL OF INFAMY #2

Apple refused to allow its products to be cloned. Apple took the view that the only way to ensure the quality of its products was to try to retain control of everything. Later this included its proprietary Macintosh operating system. For years, the company resolutely refused to license its Apple Mac operating system to other manufacturers. This meant that anyone who wanted the user-friendly Apple operating system had to buy an

217

Apple computer. It was a strategy that seemed to make sense, but only by the old rules of the game. The problem for Apple was that in terms of business model and strategic vision, it was only one generation away from the hardware dinosaur, IBM.

Says William Halal of George Washington University: "If Steve Jobs and John Sculley had understood the potential for a standardized software platform, they could now be holding the monopoly that Microsoft enjoys. And Macintosh is a better system. This illustrates the huge impact that negative decisions can have."

THE HALL OF INFAMY #3

Truth be told, Apple features prominently in the Hall of Infamy. How not to manage? Take a few years from Apple's life in the early 1990s. Error followed disaster as easily as triumph had once followed triumph. The company lost a copyright ruling in a lawsuit against Microsoft. In 1993 it launched the Newton personal assistant. The Newton flopped and CEO John Sculley left. In 1995, it was last-chance time once again. Apple launched its new laptops, but was forced to recall them after two burst into flames. Profits dropped by 48 percent. By 1996, Apple's market share was down to 5 percent, compared to 20 percent in its prime. New CEO Gil Amelio lasted 500 days. Amelio brought back Steve Jobs and then lost his job. During this time, Apple did not make many great decisions.

THE HALL OF INFAMY #4

"How about a negative that led to a positive decision?" asks leadership guru Warren Bennis. "I'm thinking of how Xerox turned down the first PC and allowed Jobs to steal it, virtually handed it to him. That legitimate steal led to the first mass marketing of a PC, and Jobs did it in daylight." Xerox's PARC research establishment had the technology; the company either did not have the will or did not see the opportunity.

THE HALL OF INFAMY #5

Xerox was not alone. "In the mid-1970s, someone came to me with an idea for what was basically the PC," Gordon Moore of Intel admits. "I personally didn't see anything useful in it, so we never gave it another thought." But then again, Intel has done quite well in other areas.

THE HALL OF INFAMY #6

A great furor was caused in the 1990s by minuscule crystals of manganese, humble pink crystals that led to an expensive and long-running war between the Anglo-Dutch giant Unilever and its traditional rival, Procter & Gamble. The chairman of Unilever's U.K. business, Sir Michael Perry, later called it "the greatest marketing setback we've seen."

While P&G and Unilever have been involved in fierce competition for many decades, the contest has always embodied a kind of Corinthian concept of good sportsmanship. This began to unravel in February 1994, when Unilever launched its new Omo Power and Persil Power detergents in three European countries. The marketing plan called for a rapid and very expensive launch in 11 European countries in quick succession.

Unilever claimed that the new product (labeled either Omo or Persil in different European countries) was a huge technological leap forward. "We always knew it would start a washing revolution. We just didn't expect it to start a war," a statement from the company later observed.

The crucial crystals in the Power products were manganese. P&G had tested manganese and found it could attack fabrics and accelerate bleaching. It had, as a result, put a stop to its research. Unilever, however, had gamely carried on, optimistic that it could eventually find a solution to the problem. It thought it had done so; in the new products manganese was used as a catalyst to increase the cleaning power of the detergent.

The launch of the new product did apparently give Unilever the leap forward it needed. P&G's new detergent, Ariel Future, was not scheduled to be launched until later in 1994. The Power detergent appeared to be highly effective in removing stains. P&G quickly began examining the ingredients of the new Unilever detergent. Its research suggested that the new Power products created holes in clothes after repeated washing. "Only Ariel washes so clean yet so safe," ran P&G's advertisements in newspapers. If this was not controversial enough, P&G also claimed that the manganese was actually retained by the clothes, so that even if they were washed in other detergents, the effect would continue. P&G's claims sparked war.

At the beginning of June, Unilever pointed to increased U.K. market share as clear evidence that it was winning the war. Even so, Unilever also confirmed that it planned to reduce the quantity of manganese in its detergent and was already making plans for a replacement product in case of disaster. P&G retaliated with claims that even at one-tenth of initial levels, the manganese would still cause abnormal wear and tear on clothes washed in the Power products.

The next front was opened when, in July, Unilever said it had a copy of the draft sales brochure and a sample of P&G's new detergent, Ariel Future, which P&G planned to launch in Germany in the autumn and later in the rest of Europe. Unilever proclaimed that its examination of the brochure and sample showed that P&G's offensive against the Power products was simply a matter of corporate pique. Unilever claimed that P&G had simply been beaten at the last.

In response, P&G claimed that Ariel Future "is not a copy-cat product but a leap-frog product," and pointed out that it would not include any manganese and none had actually been produced.

By August the battle was at its worst. Unilever attacked. It claimed that Power products were environmentally friendlier than competing products. Advertisements from P&G continued to ram the message home: "Only Ariel washes so clean yet so safe," it proclaimed, with warnings that the manganese accelerator could leave residues on clothes and continue to cause fading. P&G's advertisements led to complaints to the Advertising Standards Authority by Unilever, challenging the test results and disputing P&G's claims of Ariel's superiority.

In September the claim and counterclaim continued with an outbreak of reports. A report from the Dutch consumers' association was critical of Power, claiming that some fabrics were "damaged" in their tests.

In November P&G launched its new product, Ariel Futur (or Future in the United Kingdom). It marked, claimed P&G, "a considerable technological advance in washing powders." Backed by an $11.2 million television advertising campaign in the United Kingdom, Future hit the shops in January 1995. In the same month, Unilever announced that it was planning to launch a new flagship detergent, New Generation Persil. The new product, it said, was more effective at cleaning and less damaging than Ariel Future. Most importantly, it did not include any pink crystals.

Announcing a rise in profits to $3.81 billion in February 1995, Unilever announced it was writing off $237 million of stock, thanks to the soap war.

THE HALL OF INFAMY #7

Americans would have you believe that Eli Whitney was the first champion of the concept of producing interchangeable parts. In fact, Whitney was not the first. Eighteenth-century clockmakers realized the possibilities of interchangeable parts and so too did Honore Blanc, an eighteenth-century French gunsmith. Blanc even arranged a demonstration involving 1,000 muskets. Thomas Jefferson, then the American ambassador to France, reported from Paris on this development.

Soon Blanc was making 1,000 muskets a year for Napoleon. Interchangeable parts meant that he could use unskilled labor to make the weapons. The French government didn't like this. They proclaimed that it simply wasn't practical or sensible for people to make only a bit of a product. Craftsmanship required that individuals make the whole product. Blanc's manufacturing methods, the precursor to mass production, were unceremoniously brought to halt. If they had been allowed to continue, Henry Ford may well have been called Henri.

THE HALL OF INFAMY #8

During the 1970s, Japanese giant Matsushita developed VHS video and made the decision to license the technology. Sony developed the immeasurably better Betamax, but failed to license it. The world standard in video is VHS, and Betamax is consigned to history—all for the want of a license.

THE HALL OF INFAMY #9

Henry Ford gave the world mass production. He gave the world affordable cars. He gave his workers $5 a day. For all these reasons, Henry Ford will go down in history. But he was also only human, and he made some blunders along the way.

One of the most notable was his decision to make submarines. In 1917, as the First World War raged and U-boats were destroying Allied ships, Ford announced with due solemnity that he could "build 1,000 small submarines—a day."

The Navy was desperate and brought Ford in to build 200-foot Eagle boats. Ford, as you would expect, immediately set up a production line. In May 1918, his sub factory came into being; in July it produced its first Eagle. The goal was to produce a boat every day, a rather tame goal considering Ford's previous boast.

The Eagles produced weren't a great deal of use in fighting the Germans. Ford had figured with characteristic arrogance and no small amount of stupidity that making a boat was similar to making a car. His boats leaked. He ignored the best brains on offer at the Navy and plowed on. In the first year, 17 Eagles were produced. Ford eventually delivered his sixtieth and final Eagle in 1919. By 1939, only eight were still in use. (Having learned his maritime lesson, Ford moved on to produce planes during the Second World War, with indifferent results.)

THE HALL OF INFAMY #10

Thomas Edison's belief that iron could be extracted from low-grade ore cost him a great deal of money and proved that throwing good money after bad simply produces more bad money.

Edison, at the time, was the world's foremost inventor. In the late 1890s, he had already invented the electric light, the phonograph, and a plethora of other life-enhancing products. The idea of extracting iron from poor-quality ore was ridiculed by one publication in its editorial. It was termed "Edison's Folly." The great man took umbrage and, in doing so, quickly proved the editorial right. He poured money into his idea. Unfortunately, the opening of a new iron range led to a fall in the price of iron and Edison's dream disappeared. It was, of course, Edison who noted that genius is largely a matter of knowing what won't work.

THE HALL OF INFAMY #11

Schlitz, the American beer, is now found only occasionally among the mass of taps bearing the logos of Budweiser, Miller, Molson, and the like. But in 1974 Schlitz was America's second most popular brand of beer. It held 16 percent of the massive American market and appeared destined for a comfortable, long life. Then the brewers introduced a revolutionary new process, "accelerated batch fermentation." This saved time and money. It appeared a triumph for all concerned. The beer tasted the same; what else could matter?

The trouble was that customers didn't have faith in the new process. They believed the beer was below the standard they had come to expect. It tasted the same, but customers *believed* it wasn't the same. Schlitz's market share fell to less than a single percentage point, and the value of its name declined from more than $1 billion in 1974 to around $75 million in 1980.

THE HALL OF INFAMY #12

At the beginning of the 1990s, Hoover in the United Kingdom ran a thoroughly misguided marketing promotion that greatly damaged its credibility and cost it millions of pounds. What seemed at first a brilliant idea to boost sales—by offering free flights to Europe or the United States to any British customer who spent a minimum of $160 on Hoover products—turned into a corporate disaster. Marketing executives at Hoover miscalculated consumer tenacity, making the promotion vastly more expensive than anticipated.

The problem was brought to light not by the company, which must have known the tide of complaints was rising, but by media stories about angry customers who bought Hoover products, filled out their applications for tickets, and then heard nothing from the company. The first mistake was then exacerbated by a series of subsequent blunders. These included a failure to act quickly enough to restore customer confidence and a public relations faux pas involving a comment by a Hoover manager that customers were foolish to expect something for nothing.

In April 1993, Hoover's U.S. parent company, Maytag, announced a net loss of $10.5 million in the first quarter, after taking a special charge of $30 million to cover the unexpected cost of the free flights promotion.

THE HALL OF INFAMY #13

Charles Goodyear (1800–1860) was not one of earth's luckier inhabitants. In fact, he could fill an entire Hall of Infamy. It was not only that he was a bad businessman—which he was—but he was also just plain unlucky. He was remarkably philosophical about his lack of good fortune: "Life should not be estimated exclusively by the standard of dollars and cents. I am not disposed to complain that I have planted and others have gathered the fruits. A man has cause for regret only when he sows and no one reaps."

Goodyear developed the process of vulcanization. The process turned rubber from an adhesive and largely impractical material into one that could be used for a huge variety of purposes. Goodyear himself used rubber for more purposes than are usually contemplated. Among his many experiments were rubber hats, vests, and ties, rubber banknotes, and rubber books. Goodyear believed in rubber, but was usually a little slow about registering his patents and a bit careless about business matters.

Goodyear hardly made a cent from all his brilliant inventiveness. At one point he and his family were living in the remnants of one of his failed rubber factories on Staten Island, kept alive by eating the fish Goodyear caught. Goodyear spent a great deal of time and money trying to fend off unscrupulous pirates who stole his ideas. At one point he seemed to have won. In 1852 the U.S. Supreme Court ruled in his favor and outlawed any further infringements of Goodyear's patents. Goodyear cheerfully handed over $15,000 to his lawyer, none other than Daniel Webster. Unfortunately, the infringements continued and at his death, Goodyear had built up debts of $200,000.

It is no surprise, therefore, that the Goodyear Tire & Rubber Company, the world's largest rubber business, has no connection with Charles Goodyear at all, apart from borrowing his name. Goodyear was founded in 1898 by Frank A. Seiberling. From its first factory on the banks of the Little Cuyahoga River in East Akron, Ohio, it made horse-shoe pads, bicycle and carriage tires, sealing rings for canning, fire hose, and even rubber poker chips. Goodyear got off to an immediately prof-itable start. Its first month's sales amounted to $8,246. Charles Goodyear would have blown the lot.

THE HALL OF INFAMY #14

We won't mention the ads populated by frogs. The jury is still out on how ludicrous that campaign was. Instead, we go back to the start of Budweiser's corporate life. Quintessentially American it may be, but Budweiser's history is dogged by a decidedly un-American subtext. It was in 1876 that Anheuser-Busch decided to use the name Budweiser, after a type of beer from a place called Budweis in an obscure outpost of the Austro-Hungarian Empire. Budweis has since evolved into Ceske Budejovice in the Czech Republic. While its name and its rulers have changed, this small town retains its brewing tradition. Indeed, the mod-ern Czech company, Budejovicky Budvar, is some 700 years old. It enjoys a healthy local market. The Czechs drink beer as enthusiastically as they drink tap water; their average consumption of 160 liters a year per capita is the highest in the world. Budvar flourishes and, much to Anheuser-Busch's annoyance, has the legal right to use the Budweiser name in over 40 countries.

The legal wrangling between the American giant ("The King of Beers," according to its slogan) and the Czech minnow ("The Beer of Kings," according to its slogan) has been rumbling on for decades. The Czechs remain recalcitrant, unwilling to roll over and take the dollars offered. It is for this reason that in some countries, the Budweiser brand is marketed as Bud. An irritant perhaps, but who knows how big Budweiser might be if it had chosen a different name?

THE HALL OF INFAMY #15

Some terrible decisions sort themselves out eventually. We have already looked at how one of the worst decisions in corporate history turned into a triumph—for stockholders at least—but more misfortune lurked around the corner for Coca-Cola after the New Coke fiasco (see Greatest Decision #32).

Coca-Cola's disastrous acquisition of Columbia Pictures in 1982 proved a nightmare to manage. Synergy was notable in its absence. Yet this was one of the best deals in corporate history. In terms of sheer profit, it is difficult to match. Just a few years later, Coca-Cola sold Columbia to Sony, making a profit of nearly $1 billion. When CEO Roberto Goizueta died in 1997, the company was valued at $145 billion, compared with $4 billion when he took over the top job. Goizueta had the last laugh and proved that fortune favors the brave—even when they screw up.

THE HALL OF INFAMY #16

... And some mistaken decisions repeat themselves. In 1989, Sony bought Columbia Pictures. This seemed to cement its role as the Japanese conqueror of the Western world. It turned out to be one of the few blemishes in Sony's innovative history, the Betamax fiasco being the other. Sony eventually wrote off $3.2 billion for its movie operations. Even so, the modern Sony is a $37 billion company.

THE HALL OF INFAMY #17

American Express's travails deserve mention. An almost dysfunctional management team led by CEO James Robinson III damaged the Amex brand. Robinson's grand strategy to turn the company into a financial supermarket collapsed. In 1993, Robinson was replaced as CEO by Harvey Golub, but not before the company's Shearson Lehman brokerage subsidiary had eaten up about $4 billion in capital before being sold off.

THE HALL OF INFAMY #18

Some decisions are not bad in themselves, but are simply too little, too late. The oil crisis of the 1970s and the ensuing panic among Western companies provided a case in point. "The GM downsizing decision always struck me as highly significant," says William Halal of George Washington University, author of *The Infinite Resource*. "I was a consultant to GM for many years and I constantly heard about their various attempts to head off the energy crisis that they knew loomed ahead. They convened task forces to study it many times during the sixties and seventies, introduced two or three small cars that bombed, looked into alternative fuels, and so on. But when the OPEC oil embargo hit, they bit the bullet and decided to reduce the entire line of GM cars by 1,000 pounds each. Because GM was the powerhouse of the Industrial Age, this decision changed the entire American view of the auto and ended the age of innocence, when we had heretofore disregarded the environment and its limitations."

THE HALL OF INFAMY #19

Then there is IBM. In the 1980s, PCs became commodities, selling chiefly on price. Previously, consumers had been wooed by the brand difference offered by IBM. This came in the form of security, confidence, and quality. At one point, IBM earned 70 percent of the worldwide computer industry's profits.

When companies and consumers realized that PCs were indistinguishable, there was no need to pay extra for IBM's brand. IBM's gross profit margins fell from 55 percent in 1990 to 38 percent in 1993. Reassurance went out the window. As a result, cheap clones knocked IBM from its lofty perch.

The IBM brand was ranked third in the world in 1993; by the 1994 league tables, it was rated as having a negative value. "For twenty years IBM was in charge of the transformation agenda in the computer industry. Then the industry became driven by the vision and strategy of other companies. IBM's problems are not about implementation, but foresight," says contemporary strategy guru Gary Hamel.

The fall of IBM provides an object lesson in what not to do when handling powerful brands. Wharton's George S. Day has argued that central to IBM's fall was that it became "self-centered." IBM became distant from its customers. Customer information was poorly captured and distributed. Senior managers became ever more distant from what was happening in the marketplace. (One critic compared IBM to a music publishing company run by deaf people.)

In addition, IBM's undoubted centers of excellence existed in isolation. The company continued to sustain superb standards, but lacked any means of delivering such excellence on a broader scale. IBM also began to concentrate on cost reduction to achieve short-term financial results, rather than focusing on long-term development.

Day also contends that IBM fell into what he calls "the customer compulsion trap," this time in the early 1990s. In effect, IBM sought to redress the balance by listening to each and every one of its customers. The result was confusion and disillusionment. At the beginning of the 1990s, IBM stood at the corporate precipice. Big Blue, the symbol of American corporate might, recorded massive losses and seemed too out of touch with the marketplace to make a comeback.

THE HALL OF INFAMY #20

The wisdom of this decision is open to question and debate, but there is no doubting its impact. In the 1880s, Frederick Taylor decided to time each and every movement of workers at the Midvale Steel Company, where he was chief engineer. This led to the creation of scientific management and the twentieth century's preoccupation with management by measurement.

Taylor was the first and purest believer in command and control. In his 1911 book, *The Principles of Scientific Management,* Taylor laid out his route to improved performance:

1. Find, say, 10 or 15 different men (preferably in as many separate establishments and different parts of the country) who are especially skillful in doing the particular work analyzed.

2. Study the exact series of elementary operations or motions which each of these men uses in doing the work being investigated, as well as the implements each man uses.

3. Study with a stopwatch the time required to make each of these elementary movements and then select the quickest way of doing each element of the work.

4. Eliminate all false movements, slow movements and useless movements.

5. … [C]ollect into one series the quickest and best movements as well as the best implements.

Having identified every single movement and action involved in doing something, Taylor could determine the optimum time required to complete a task. Armed with this information, the manager could determine whether a person was doing the job well.

There can be no doubting the impact of Taylor's thinking on a wider audience. Mussolini and Lenin were admirers, but so were many thousands of ordinary businesspeople. Astonishingly, a talk by Taylor in New York in 1914 attracted an audience of 69,000. Scientific management had an effect throughout the world. A Japanese engineer translated *The Principles of Scientific Management;* in Japan, it became *Secrets for Eliminating Futile Work and Increasing Production.* The Japanese book was a best-seller, foreshadowing Japanese willingness to embrace the latest Western thinking.

Right or wrong, moral or amoral, Taylor's view of the future of industry was accurate. "In the past the man was first. In the future the system will be first," he said, and so it proved. Central to this metamorphosis, however, was the role of managers. Scientific management elevated the role of managers and negated the role of workers. Armed with their scientifically gathered information, managers dictated terms. "Science, not rule of thumb," said Taylor. The decisions of supervisors, based on experience and intuition, were no longer considered to be important. Employees were not allowed to have any ideas or sense of responsibility. Their job was simply to perform tasks as delineated by the all-seeing and all-knowing manager. The question must be whether managers have justified their promotion to center stage.

THE HALL OF INFAMY #21

In the late 1960s the British newspaper, the *News of the World*, was owned by the Carr family, with 27 percent of the company shares. Unfortunately for them, a quarter of the company's shares were in the hands of a family cousin who wanted out. First on the scene to buy the shares was Robert Maxwell.

The Czech-born Maxwell was not a welcome suitor. He was everything the Carrs detested. Unpleasant nationalism quickly surfaced. "That foreigner" is how the Carrs described Maxwell. The trouble for them was that there weren't any members of the British aristocracy willing to stump up the cash for their saucy scandal sheet. Their unlikely knight in shining armor was Rupert Murdoch. Somehow, the Australian was deemed less foreign than Maxwell, who had lived in the country for decades, had been a member of Parliament, and had won the Military Cross.

Blind prejudice gave Murdoch an entrée into international newspaper publishing. The British establishment closed ranks against Maxwell and welcomed Murdoch as an honorary member. Murdoch played his part brilliantly. He wined and dined. He smoothed a potentially difficult path. The Carrs felt reassured. Murdoch's masterly move was to ask Sir William Carr to remain as chairman, with his nephew as joint managing director with Murdoch. The deal was made on the premise that the Carr's involvement in the newspaper would continue.

The prize was won at an Extraordinary General Meeting at the Connaught Rooms near London's Covent Garden on January 2, 1969. Maxwell told Murdoch that he had caught "a big fish with a very small hook." For once, Maxwell was not exaggerating. Murdoch could not have afforded to match Maxwell's offer and it was only through various exchanges of shares that Murdoch's deal was possible. The Carrs actually lost around $4 million in accepting their knight in shining armor rather than Maxwell. For Murdoch it was a lucky break. It was the deal he needed to make the leap from national newspaper proprietor to international media kingpin. His orbit of influence expanded overnight.

Soon after, Murdoch wrote to Sir William Carr, informing him that the joint managing director arrangement was not tenable and a new chairman would also be a good idea. After promising not to seek to own the newspaper outright, six months later Murdoch sought control, buying the shares of the Carrs' cousin.

The Carr family lost control of their newspaper and £2 million—all through their bigoted decision.

INDEX